Focus: Take A Closer Look
Published by Orange, a division of The reThink Group, Inc.
5870 Charlotte Lane, Suite 300
Cumming, GA 30040 U.S.A.

Other Orange products are available online and direct from the publisher. Visit our
website at www.WhatIsOrange.org for more resources like these.

ISBN: 978-1-63570-098-5
©2020 The reThink Group, Inc.

reThink Conceptual Team: Reggie Joiner, Kristen Ivy, Mike Clear, Donny Joiner, Candice
Wynn, Elloa Davis, Ben Crawshaw, Sarah Anderson
Lead Writer: Holly Crawshaw
Editing: Lauren Terrell
Art Direction: Sharon VanRossum
Project Manager: Nate Brandt
Design, Layout, and Illustration: Jacob Hunt
Printed in the United States of America
First Edition 2020
1 2 3 4 5 6 7 8 9 10

03/08/20

INTRODUCTION

Let's talk about the obvious: you're holding a book.

I don't know what you thought about books before today, but here's the deal . . . this isn't just *any* book. Nope. This book is different. This book can teach *you* to be different. It can teach you to see things other people can't see.

No, I'm serious!

This book is all about a little word with a big meaning: *faith*.

Faith means trusting in what you can't see because of what you can see.

It's okay if that doesn't make sense yet. Because together, we're going to conduct an experiment. An experiment to investigate what it means to have faith.

And like with all good experiments, we need a plan—a method.

Here's how this is going to work:

Four days a week, you'll read one devotional entry.

On the fifth day, there's a Challenge that you can do or skip. (But I don't think you'll want to miss out on these!)

Oh, and make sure to keep track of your Focus Decoder. You can find it at the back of this book! With it, you can check out cool facts or helpful tips throughout the book. Put it somewhere safe! In fact, keeping this book along with a pen or pencil in the same place as your decoder is a great way to make the most of our time together.

If you miss a day, don't give up. Just start back where you left off the next chance you get.

Want to know my hypothesis? What I think is going to happen? By the end of this book, you're going to know more, understand more—but more importantly, you're going to *see* more.

All you have to do is *focus*.

. . . oh, and you have to turn the page!

HEBREWS 11:1-12:3

DAY 1

YOU CAN KNOW JESUS EVEN THOUGH YOU'VE NEVER SEEN HIM.

Focus.

Is that a word you've ever heard before? Maybe your dad was trying to get you to concentrate on your math homework, but a new episode of your favorite show just dropped on YouTube and you couldn't add one more decimal until you saw what happened next.

FOCUS.

Or maybe your soccer coach caught you daydreaming about what you were going to have for dinner.

FOOOO-CUUUUUUSSS!

Or your best friend stopped in the middle of their story about the new skateboard trick they landed because you were staring into space, wondering if ants sleep at night or not.

Focus.

But what does that really mean? To focus? In the space below, define "focus" in your own words:

- -

- -

- -

Put a check mark beside any of the following words that you used:

☐ Attention   ☐ Distraction
☐ Mind   ☐ Thoughts
☐ Eyes

Since the name of this book is *Focus*, we should probably agree on a definition. For us, let's define focus as . . .

Taking a closer look.

In other words, wherever your mind was before—or wherever your *eyes* were before—you move them back to what matters most. When you focus on something, you give it your attention. All of your attention.

DECODE IT!

Which birds of prey can quickly shift focus, allowing them to "zoom in" on their prey with their eyes?

This week, we want you to focus on the idea of *faith*.

We've already said that faith is trusting in what you can't see because of what you can see. So how are you supposed to do that? How are you supposed to focus on something you can't see?

You focus on what you *can* see.

Think of yourself as an investigator. If you were trying to solve a crime that no one witnessed, you would look for evidence of what happened. You'd look at what you *can* see to tell you what you *can't* see.

In the Bible, we hear about a guy named Paul. Early in his life, Paul hated Christians. His job was to find people who followed Jesus and punish them. But then one day, God spoke to Paul and his life was changed forever. He began to have faith.

We're going to learn a lot about Paul in this book, but for right now, all you need to know is that Paul's faith grew and grew until he had big, big faith. People couldn't believe how big Paul's faith was. The author of Hebrews explains faith like this:

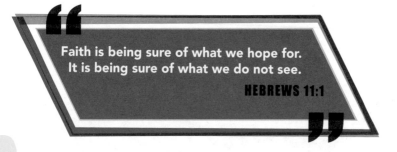

> Faith is being sure of what we hope for.
> It is being sure of what we do not see.
>
> **HEBREWS 11:1**

If we want to have big, big faith, we can look at what we *do* see to be sure of what we *do not* see. You do this all the time! Have you ever seen the leaves moving when there's a breeze? You can't see the wind. But you know it exists because of what you *can* see.

Even though we can't see Jesus, we *can* see evidence that He exists.

If you can, go outside. If you can't, find a window to look out of. Draw a sketch of what you see. (Stick figures are totally allowed!)

See that? He did all of that. Created all of that! The people, the trees—even the stuff the buildings and houses are made of. He made all of it. When it feels hard to have faith, look at what you can see to believe in what you can't see.

DAY 2

FAITH IS...
ONE WAY WE CAN CONNECT WITH GOD.

Did you know that in 2003, scientists discovered another planet? Sure, it's a dwarf planet (meaning it's too small to be an actual planet, but too big to be classified as anything else).[2] But it's a super cool dwarf planet. Check out these stats on the dwarf planet Haumea:

- About the same size as Pluto
- Has two moons
- Spins super fast on its axis
- Is shaped like a football
- Takes 285 Earth-years to orbit the sun
- Is encircled by a ring of particles[3]

Isn't that incredible? A football shaped dwarf-planet that spins super fast? What's not to love?!

What if you could create your own planet or dwarf-planet?

What would you name it? _

What shape would it be? _

What would be its best feature? _

Isn't it fascinating that even though scientists and astronomers have been studying the galaxy for centuries, they are still discovering new things?

That's because plenty of things exist that we can't see. In fact, scientists estimate that there are at least 100 billion undiscovered stars and planets in our Milky Way Galaxy alone.[4] In their own way, these scientists have faith—they believe in what they can't see (undiscovered planets and stars) because of what they can see (evidence, research, and context clues).

The author of Hebrews tells us one very important fact about faith:

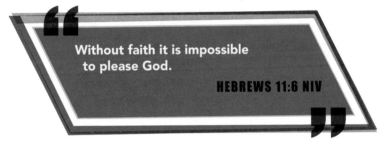

Without faith it is impossible to please God.

HEBREWS 11:6 NIV

You want to know how to connect with God? Have faith in Him. Believe that He created you, loves you, and wants you to be in His family forever.

You are one of God's favorite things, ever!

Maybe you have no problem believing in God. Or maybe you still have questions. That's okay; keep reading!

Spend a couple of minutes talking to God. Ask Him to help you focus on what matters most. Ask Him to show you evidence that He is real. Ask Him to help you believe in what you can't see because of what you can see.

BONUS ACTIVITY

Grab a device (smartphone, tablet, etc.) and download the app **Night Sky**. (Always get a parent's permission before using technology or downloading new content!) Using the app, move your device's camera around to see which stars, planets, and constellations surround you. You can know all this without even walking outside!

Everything you see didn't happen on accident. God placed each and every star and planet exactly where they are on purpose. When you believe that, when you have faith in Him, nothing gets God more excited!

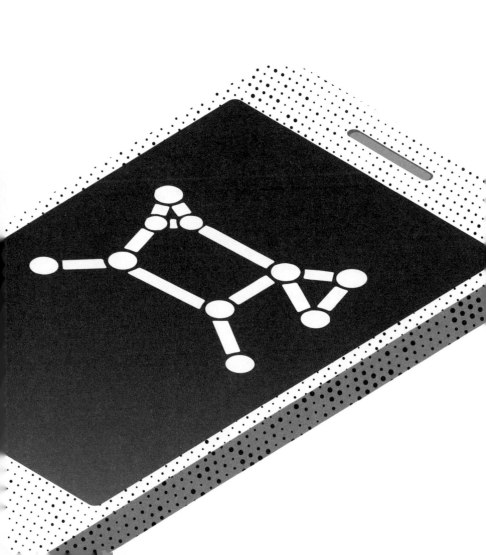

DAY 3

FAITH IS...
SOMETHING THAT MOVES
US INTO ACTION.

Have you ever been to the doctor and had them place two fingers on your wrist while watching a clock? They were taking your pulse—measuring the number of times your heart beats per minute.

Have you ever seen your own heart? Nope. Do you believe that you have one? Yup. Because of the evidence: you're walking, talking, breathing, and living.

Your pulse is even *more* proof that you have a heart. Did you know there are lots of ways to take your pulse? Let's try a few together!

You're going to need a watch or timer for this activity. Go grab one now!

First, take your *Radial Pulse.*[5]

Place your middle and pointer finger from one hand on the wrist of your other hand, just below your thumb and palm.

Once you feel your pulse, start the timer for 60 seconds.

Count the number of pulses and record it below.

_ _ _ _ _ _ _ _ _ beats per minute

Next, take your *Carotid Pulse.*

Place your middle and pointer finger on the side of your windpipe just below your jawbone. You may have to move your fingers around a little until you easily feel your heart beating.

Once you feel your pulse, start the timer for 60 seconds.

Count the number of pulses and record it below.

_ _ _ _ _ _ _ _ _ beats per minute

This last method is the coolest one by far. Take your *Pedal Pulse.*

Place your middle and pointer finger on the highest point of bone that runs across the top of your foot.

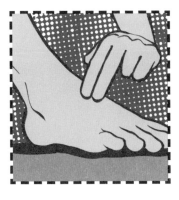

Once you feel your pulse, start the timer for 60 seconds.

Count the number of pulses and record it below.

_ _ _ _ _ _ _ _ _ beats per minute

The heart is a pretty cool organ.
Check out these facts about the heart:

- The average heart in an adult is the size of a fist.
- Your heart will beat around 115,000 times per day.
- Your heart pumps about 2,000 gallons of blood every day.
- Your heart is controlled by an electrical system called the cardiac conduction system.
- The heart can keep beating even when it's disconnected from the body.[6]

That last one sounds a little freaky, right? But it's true! The heart is one of the most important organs in the body.

But "heart" has more than one meaning, right? Heart can be our actual, physical heart, but it can also mean the place our feelings, emotions, and thoughts live. When we're kind to others, it's said that we "have a good heart."

In Hebrews we read about all the people from God's Story who had big, big faith. Each one of these people had something in common. Check it out:

> Abel had faith. So he brought God a better offering . . .
>
> HEBREWS 11:4a
>
> Noah had faith. So he built an ark . . .
>
> HEBREWS 11:7a
>
> Abraham had faith. So he obeyed God . . .
>
> HEBREWS 11:8a
>
> Isaac had faith. So he blessed . . .
>
> HEBREWS 11:20a
>
> Joseph had faith. So he spoke . . .
>
> HEBREWS 11:22a

See a pattern? Each person who had faith *did* something because of their faith. Faith is something that makes people *move*. It makes people act. It makes people treat others a different way—a *better* way.

If you want to grow your faith, one place to start is by being a kind person. Does that mean you have to be in a good mood every minute of every day? Of course not. It simply means that you treat people the way you want to be treated.

Who is someone you can show kindness to tomorrow?

- -

How can you show them kindness?

- -

- -

- -

Grow your faith by having a heart—a heart that loves and respects others.

DAY 4

FAITH IS . . .
SOMETHING WE ALREADY
HAVE EVERY DAY.

Let's take a quick survey:

Favorite song: _

_ _

Favorite singer/band: _

Worst song you've ever heard: _ _ _ _ _ _ _ _ _ _ _ _ _ _ _ _ _ _ _

_ _

Song you know every word to: _ _ _ _ _ _ _ _ _ _ _ _ _ _ _ _ _ _ _

_ _

Song you're embarrassed that you know every word to:

_ _

_ _

Music is amazing, right? Think about it.

There's music for every mood: exercising, relaxing, walking to the bus stop, hanging out with friends. Music can make us remember a different time, like how that song you played over and over again last summer still reminds you of the beach. Music can say things that we can't. Life without music wouldn't be nearly as fun.

Have you ever thought about what makes music . . . music?

All music is made up of musical notes. Notes can be made by any type of instrument[7]—voices, guitars, flutes, pianos, xylophones. And when you repeat those notes over and over again in a pattern, you get music!

When you think about it, music is really just different sounds. Sound. Now, *sound* is pretty cool. Sound is a type of energy made by vibrations. When any object vibrates, it causes movement of air particles. These particles bump into the particles close to them, which makes them vibrate too, causing waves in the air that you can actually hear.[8]

DECODE IT!

What sound do scientists think may alter the structure of the brain?[9]

Sound is something we don't *see* every day, but it is something we *have faith in* every day.

- When you open your mouth, you believe you'll be able to speak.
- When you plug in your headphones and put them on, you believe you'll hear your favorite song as soon as you press play.
- When you turn on your favorite YouTube episode, you believe the volume will increase when you press that button.

Come up with your own example of when you have faith in sound:

When I . . .

- -

- -

- -

I believe that . . .

- -

- -

- -

Sound is something you believe in even though you can't see it.

In Hebrews we read . . .

> . . . So let us throw off everything that stands in our way . . . And let us keep on running the race marked out for us. Let us keep looking to Jesus. He is the one who started this journey of faith.
>
> **HEBREWS 12:1-2b**

Since we already believe in so many things that we can't see, why do you think it's sometimes hard to have faith in Jesus? List a few of your own reasons below. (And if it's easy for you to have faith, think of some reasons it may be challenging for others.)

1. _____

_____

2. _____

_____

3. _____

_____

The author of Hebrews tells us that we should "throw off" everything that stands in the way of having faith.

Copy down each of those reasons onto the sheets on the next page. Tear those pieces out of this book and make one, giant ball. (Feel free to use your own scrap paper to make it bigger!)

Now, throw that ball of reasons. No, seriously. Give it a huge, heaving, with-all-your-might throw. Slam it against the wall. Smash it into the floor. Use a book like a bat and hit the ball as if you're in the World Series and the entire game rests on your shoulders.

When you're finished "throwing off" your reasons not to have faith, spend a couple of minutes talking to God. Ask Him to help your faith grow bigger and bigger. Tell Him that you have thrown off all the reasons you had before not to have faith. Then, ask Him to help you have faith in what you can't see, because of what you can see.

DECODE IT!

When was the first mention of magnifying lenses in recorded history?[10]

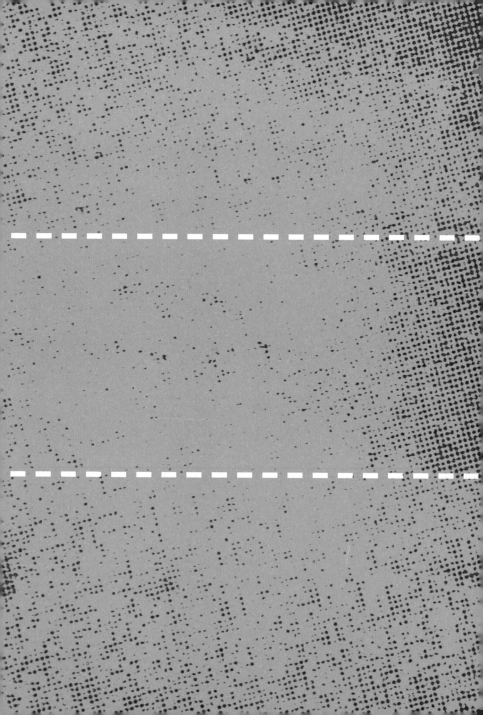

CHALLENGE 1

This week, we've learned a lot of things about what faith is. What's the *main* thing you learned this week that you don't want to forget? (Look back at the bottom lines if you need a reminder!)

- -

- -

Ready to do a little experiment? You probably have the following supplies around your house:

- Dry rice (or dry cereal, dry noodles, sugar, salt— any dry, lightweight food!)
- Sheet of paper
- Rubber band (or hair tie)
- Cup
- Large, metal spoon (Make sure an adult is cool with you banging this around.)
- Baking sheet (Ask an adult to show you what this is if you're unsure!)
- Bonus: a speaker you can use to play music

On Day 4 of this week, we talked about sound. We said that sound is a type of energy made by vibrations. While you can't really *see* sound, you know it exists because you can observe its effects. For example, you can *hear* it.

But today, you're going to *see* sound's effects.

Step 1
Place the sheet of paper on top of the cup's opening.

Step 2
Fold down the paper over the cup's opening and secure it using the rubber band.

Step 3
Place a spoonful of dry rice on top of the sheet of paper, spreading it out.

Step 4
Warn your family that things are about to get loud—really, really loud. (You should probably make sure it's cool with a grown-up, while you're at it.)

Step 5
Using the metal spoon, bang the baking sheet close to the rice **without touching the rice.**

BONUS STEP
Hold your speaker close to the rice and blast your favorite jam.

Write down what happens to the rice:

\- -

\- -

Any hypotheses (guesses) on why the rice moves when you bang the baking sheet?

\- -

\- -

You can't *see* the sounds you're making, but you can see their effects.

In the same way, you can't see Jesus, but you can see all that He has done for you and for others.

Our bottom line this week is **you can know Jesus even though you've never seen Him.**

DECODE IT!

The banging and the music causes what to move through air, causing the rice to dance?

What are some things Jesus has done for you or for your family?
(Think: Do you have a warm bed to sleep in at night? Do you
have food to eat? Friends? A healthy body?)

1. _____

_____

2. _____

_____

3. _____

_____

Remember, faith is trusting in what you can't see because of
what you can see.

WEEK 2

PAUL
RECOMES A
BELIEVER

ACTS 9:1-9

DAY 1

KNOWING JESUS CHANGES THE WAY YOU SEE EVERYTHING.

Focus on this lightbulb and count slowly to thirty.

Now, look at the center of the square below.

What did you see inside the square? Was it a glowing light bulb? C R A Z Y, right?

The eyes are an incredible organ. Check this out:
- **The human eye can detect the difference between over 10 million colors.**
- **Our eyes stay the same size our entire lives while our noses and ears keep growing.**
- **The human eye blinks an average of 4.2 MILLION times a year.**
- **Pirates wore earrings because they thought it would improve their eyesight.[1]**

Okay, maybe that last fact is a little weird, but it's true! The ability to see is a big deal.

But our eyes can sometimes play tricks on us—make us see something that isn't there or *not* see something that is there. When this happens, it's called an *optical illusion*. Like the lightbulb illustration, you saw a glowing lightbulb in an empty square. Optical illusions make us believe the impossible is possible.

Speaking of the impossible being possible, I can't wait to tell you more about Paul, the guy we talked about in Week 1. But you can't learn about Paul until you meet Saul.

DECODE IT!

What's the fastest muscle in the human body?

Saul was a bad dude. In fact, he makes the villains in movies look like teddy bears. Only, Saul was a real-life person. Check this out:

> Meanwhile, Saul continued to oppose the Lord's followers. He said they would be put to death. He went to the high priest. He asked the priest for letters to the synagogues in Damascus. He wanted to find men and women who belonged to the Way of Jesus. The letters would allow him to take them as prisoners to Jerusalem.
>
> **ACTS 9:1-2**

That's right. Saul's job was to find Jesus followers and punish them. He had just received permission to travel to a town called Damascus and search for Jesus followers to take them as his prisoners.

Then there was Paul. Paul was a man who went through a lot of pain, hurt, and hard times just to tell people about Jesus. He dedicated his entire life to start churches and help other people start churches. A lot of people say that Paul is the most famous Christian to ever live.

If you're wearing socks, reach down and hang on to them because I'm about to knock them off:

Saul is the same person as Paul.

Huh?
Whaaaa?
Excuse me?

Yup.

See, Saul/Paul met Jesus and everything about him changed. He went from punishing Jesus followers to *being* a Jesus follower!

Think about someone super important in your life—someone who has helped you see things differently. It could be a teacher, a coach, a small group leader, or a friend.

Write their name here: _

Now, write down 3 ways your life would be different if you'd never met that person.

1. _

_ _

2. _

_ _

3. _

_ _

Knowing people can change the way we see things. But knowing *Jesus* changes the way we see everything.

DAY 2

KNOWING JESUS CHANGES THE WAY YOU SEE SIN.

Find a mirror and focus on the very center of your eyes. See that black circle? That's called your pupil. Your pupils may be small, but they have a super important job.

Go to a windowless room. (Take this book with you!) If the room doesn't have a mirror, take one of those with you, too. Now, turn off the light and close the door so there is just enough light to see your pupils. As the room gets darker, what happens to your pupils?

They got _ .

Now turn on the light, focusing on the size of your pupils again.

They got _ .

In the dark, your pupils grow to their maximum size to capture as much light as possible.[2] In bright light, your pupils get smaller to prevent your eyes from getting too much light.[3]

Remember our friend Paul? Something happened to his eyes—something that you're going to have to read to believe. (And don't forget: Paul = Saul.)

Saul is a bad guy in this story. He and a bunch of guys are going to a city called Damascus to find Jesus followers to throw them into jail.

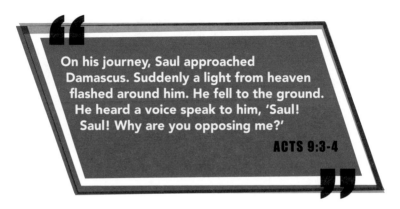

> On his journey, Saul approached Damascus. Suddenly a light from heaven flashed around him. He fell to the ground. He heard a voice speak to him, 'Saul! Saul! Why are you opposing me?'
>
> **ACTS 9:3-4**

Picture this . . .

You're walking down a road, focused on your mission. Then, out of nowhere, there's a flash of light in the sky. Not only that, but a voice saying, "Saul, why are you against me?"

If you were Saul, what would your first thought have been?

If you said, "Why is the sky flashing and why is the air talking?" you'd be a lot like me. I would have panicked. Ran. Cried. Hidden under my covers and hugged my stuffed bunny.

Saul said, "Who are you, Lord?"

Then the voice replied, "I am Jesus."

I think Saul *knew* who was talking to him before he even asked. Maybe I'm the only one, but I think Saul had started to rethink the choices he was making. I think deep down, Saul knew that punishing people for following Jesus was wrong.

You'll have to wait to hear what happened next, but for now, I want you to focus on your own life.

Have you ever done something that you knew was wrong, but you did it anyway? We all have. Maybe you were unkind to a friend, you lied to your teacher, or disrespected your parents. When we do things we know are wrong, that's called *sin*.

Maybe that's the first time you've heard that word, maybe it isn't. But when we think about *sin*, we might think about really bad, terrible, big things people do that are wrong—like stealing or lying. But really, sin is anything we do that we know we aren't supposed to. Unfortunately, we all sin. But there's good news. We can talk to God when we've done something wrong, and know that He will always forgive us. Then, with His help, we can make the right choice next time.

DECODE IT!

The things we do that we know are wrong are called . . .

We'll talk more about sin later in this book, but for now, think about something you have done that you knew was wrong. Spend a few minutes talking to God. Tell Him what you did. Ask Him to forgive you. Ask Him to help you make the right choice next time.

DAY 3

KNOWING JESUS CHANGES YOUR FOCUS.

Grab a sheet of paper and roll it into a long tube. Using your right hand, hold it up in front of your right eye, kind of like you're looking through a telescope. Keep both eyes open and focus on looking forward.

Now for the cool part.

Take your left hand (the one not holding the tube), and hold it up in front of your left eye (the eye that is *not* looking through the tube). Keep this hand open with your palm facing your face. Move that hand until the side of it is touching the side of the tube.[4]

WHAT? DO YOU SEE THAT?

It's crazy, right? It actually looks like the tube of paper is going *through* your left hand. (By the way, if your tube of paper is *actually* going through your hand . . . you may have read the directions wrong.)

How does that happen? It's another optical illusion.

Your brain takes information from both of your eyes to create one single picture. One eye sees the hole and one eye sees your hand, so the picture that your brain sees is a hole in your hand. Sometimes, our eyes can play tricks on our brain.

Let's get back to our story—the one with Saul. Saul was traveling to Damascus to find Jesus-followers so he could throw them in jail. Then suddenly, he saw light flashing around him in the sky. Maybe he thought *his* eyes were playing tricks on his brain. But they weren't . . . and his eyes were about to see something even *more* confusing.

> On his journey, Saul approached Damascus. Suddenly a light from heaven flashed around him. He fell to the ground. He heard a voice speak to him, 'Saul! Saul! Why are you opposing me?'
>
> 'Who are you, Lord?' Saul asked.
>
> 'I am Jesus,' he replied. 'I am the one you are opposing. Now get up and go into the city. There you will be told what you must do.'
>
> The men traveling with Saul stood there. They weren't able to speak. They had heard the sound. But they didn't see anyone. Saul got up from the ground. He opened his eyes, but he couldn't see. So they led him by the hand into Damascus. For three days he was blind. He didn't eat or drink anything.
>
> **ACTS 9:3-9**

So, not only did Saul see light and hear a voice, but the guys he was traveling with did, too. So, no, this was no trick. This was Jesus talking to Saul—out loud, for everyone to hear.

Then Jesus gave Saul clear instructions to go into the city and wait to be told what to do next.

When Saul tried to open his eyes again, he couldn't see. His eyes weren't playing tricks on him this time, either. In fact, the guys he was with had to lead him into the city by his hand. Saul was blind.

Think about this . . .

Why would Jesus go through all this trouble to get Saul's attention? What do you think Jesus was trying to get Saul to focus on?

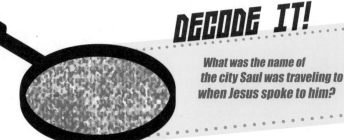

DECODE IT!

What was the name of the city Saul was traveling to when Jesus spoke to him?

Did you know that Jesus cares about you and your life just as much as He cared about Saul and Saul's life? Did you know that Jesus wants your attention and your focus to be on Him? How does that make you feel?

- -

- -

Talk to God for a few minutes and give Him your full attention. In fact, while you pray, focus on nothing else but your words to Him. Turn off all technology. Put on headphones, if you have them. Play some music without words. If it helps, write out your prayer, word-for-word. Or, close your eyes. Give God all your focus.

DAY 4

KNOWING JESUS CHANGES HOW YOU SEE YOURELF.

Have you ever played connect-the-dots? Maybe you think you've outgrown it, but connect-the-dots can still be pretty cool.

Check out the image to the right. What does that look like to you?

- -

- -

(There is no right answer here. If you said *an ice cream cone turned upside down*, that works.)

Doesn't look like much, does it?
Wait until you see what happens.

Go ahead and connect each same-numbered dot. (Draw a line between 1 and 1, 2 and 2 . . . you get the idea.)

What do you see now?

- -

- -

Okay. Maybe you still see an upside-down ice cream cone. But if you look at it just right, it also appears to be a set of railroad tracks disappearing into the distance.

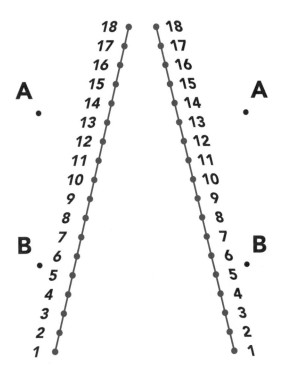

Let's keep going. On the image above, connect the letters A to A and B to B. Which line is longer? Circle your response:

A to A   **B to B**

That was a trick question because the lines are the exact same length. Line A to A may look longer than line B to B, but that's just another trick-of-the-eye, or an optical illusion.

Remember Saul? Last we checked in with Saul, he was experiencing some issues with his vision as well. Only, his problems were way more serious than mistaking one line as longer than another.

Saul and some other men were on their way to Damascus to find some Jesus-followers to take as prisoners. Then, a light flashed and Jesus spoke to Saul. Jesus asked Saul why he was against Him. In that moment, Saul lost the ability to see! When we left our story yesterday, Saul was being taken by the hand and walked into the city by his friends.

He had been blind for three days when God spoke to another man, named Ananias. God told Ananias to find Saul and pray for his eyes. Ananias had heard of Saul and was sort of afraid to go. (I would be, too! Saul was a scary dude!) But he obeyed God anyway.

When Ananias found Saul, he placed his hands on him.

> 'Brother Saul,' he said, 'you saw the Lord Jesus. He appeared to you on the road as you were coming here. He has sent me so that you will be able to see again.'
>
> **ACTS 9:17b**

After Ananias prayed for Saul, something fell out of Saul's eyes. Something like . . . scales! Have you ever seen a snake shed its skin? If you have, what they shed is probably a lot like the scales that fell out of Saul's eyes.

But guess what? SAUL COULD SEE AGAIN!

Jesus had spoken to Saul and had gotten his attention and focus. Not only that, but now Saul had *faith*.

When Saul met Jesus, everything about him changed. The way he spent his time changed. The way he spoke changed. Who he hung out with changed.

He became a man who had faith in Jesus and wanted to tell as many people about Him as possible.

What is something about you that you'd like to change? Maybe you . . .

- **are impatient.**
- **don't like to share.**
- **get angry easily.**
- **have trouble controlling what you say.**
- **don't always tell the truth.**
- **don't get along with your stepdad or your little sister.**

Write your response below:

- -

We all have things we want to get better at. Having something to work on doesn't make you a bad person, but it does give you a goal to work toward.

For the rest of this week, put a little focus on getting better at the response you gave above. Pick one thing you can do to start changing that thing for the better, and then go do it!

CHALLENGE 2

This week, we've learned how knowing Jesus changes the way you see everything. What's the *main* thing you learned this week that you don't want to forget? (Look back at the bottom lines if you need a reminder!)

- -

- -

The jumble of words below can be organized to state our definition of faith. Try to rewrite the sentence so it makes sense.

in you see see you can what of Trust can't what because.

- -

- -

Ready to do a little experiment? Let's see how good you are at creating your own optical illusions.

- **1 Quarter**
- **1 Rubber band**
- **1 Ring**
- **1 Pair of scissors**
- **1 Sheet of paper**

- **1 Marker**
- **1 Glass**
- **1 Cup of water (can be glass or plastic)**

Have you ever been to a magic show? Maybe you saw a lady get sawed in half or a rabbit was pulled from a hat. SPOILER ALERT: It's not really magic. (But you probably already knew that.) What you're seeing are optical illusions—tricks played on your brain and eyes to make you believe that what you're seeing is possible.

Today, you're going to learn how to create a few optical illusions of your own.

Let's start with the quarter.

Step 1
Hold your right palm open and place the coin on your second and third finger.

Step 2
Now, pretend that you're placing the coin in your left hand. But instead of actually moving the coin, use your thumb to press it into your second and third fingers on your right hand, keeping it there.

Step 3
Hold up your left hand, making a fist as if you're gripping the coin. Wave your left fist around in the air, drawing your audience's attention away from where the coin is hidden.

Step 4
Now it's time for the big reveal! Open your right hand, and it appears the coin has mysteriously gone from one hand to the other.

Let's move on to the ring and the rubber band.

Step 1
Use the scissors to snip the rubber band.

Step 2
Place the ring in the middle of the rubber band.

Step 3
Hold one end of the rubber band just slightly higher than the other end.

Step 4
Ever-so-slightly, stretch out the rubber band. Watch as the ring appears to move up the band on its own!

Ready for one more optical illusion?
Grab the glass, cup of water, paper, and marker.

Step 1
On the paper, draw two thick arrows, one pointing to the left and one pointing to the right.

Step 2
Place the paper on a level surface, against a wall. (For example, on your kitchen counter against the wall.)

Step 3
Place the glass a few inches in front of the paper.

Step 4
Now, pour the water from the cup into the glass. Watch as the arrows seem to change direction!

There you go! Now you have a few tricks (optical illusions) up your own sleeves!

Let me ask you this: what do optical illusions have to do with faith?

Faith means to trust in what you can't see because of what you can see. But if our eyes can play tricks on us, can we always believe in what we see?

That's where *focus* comes in. Focus on the things that matter most. Focus on the people who matter most.

When you focus on . . .

Who God is (A big, loving Father)
Who Jesus is (A friend forever)
Everything that faith in Him gives you (Hope in heaven)

. . . you start to see Jesus every day, in little and big ways. And your faith will grow and grow and grow.

What's one thing, person, or hobby that has had a lot of your focus this week?

– – – – – – – – – – – – – – – – – –

– – – – – – – – – – – – – – – – – –

What's one way you can give
more of your focus to Jesus
next week?

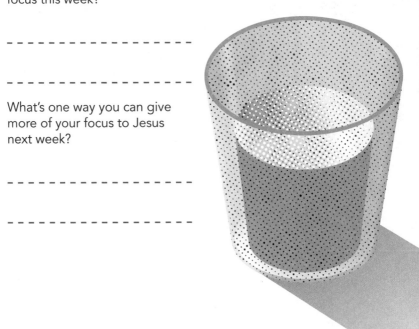

– – – – – – – – – – – – – – – – – –

– – – – – – – – – – – – – – – – – –

WEEK 9
ANANIAS
HELPS
PAUL

DAY 1

KNOWING JESUS CAN HELP YOU FACE YOUR FEARS.

Let's play a game!

Fill in the blanks below with the first idea that pops into your head.

If I had the ability to fly, the first place I would fly would be . . .

- -

If I could travel to any country besides my own, I would go to . . .

- -

If I could trade places with any person for one day, I would trade places with . . .

- -

If I could give a family member any gift imaginable, I would give them . . .

- -

If I could change anything about the world right now, I would change . . .

- -

It's fun to imagine what we would do or have or change, isn't it? It's fun to think about the "what ifs."

But what happens when our "what ifs" aren't so fun? What happens when we start wondering "what if" about things that make us nervous, afraid, or scared?

What if my grandma doesn't get better?
What if my mom doesn't find a new job?
What if my parents get a divorce?

Those "what ifs" aren't fun to think about at all. Because those "what ifs" are based on our fears.

Everybody has fears—even adults. But there is something we can do to face our fears. There's some*one* we can ask for help.

More on that later.

Let's get back to Saul, whose entire life changed when he met Jesus. There was another person involved with Saul's story, a man named Ananias.

God talked to Ananias through a vision. What's a vision? Well, it's sort of like a dream. And in this vision, God told Ananias to help Saul. Here's what Ananias said back to God:

> 'Lord,' Ananias answered, 'I've heard many reports about this man. They say he has done great harm to your holy people in Jerusalem. Now he has come here to arrest all those who worship you. The chief priests have given him authority to do this.'
>
> **ACTS 9:13-14**

Picture this: God tells you to go help someone; only that "someone" is a super scary dude. Think of the "what ifs" . . .

What if he arrests me?
What if he hurts me?
What if he hurts my family?

Ananias had fears. But they were fears he was able to face. How? You'll have to read on. For now, think about some of your own fears.

Top 3 Scariest Things Ever:

1. _

_ _

2. _

_ _

3. _

_ _

Want to know how you face those and other fears? Meet me back here tomorrow!

DECODE IT!

Trypanophobia
is the fear of what?

DAY 2

WHEN YOU'RE AFRAID, REMEMBER GOD IS WITH YOU.

What's the scariest movie, book, or story you've ever seen, read, or heard?

- -

What made it scary?

- -

- -

- -

How did your heart feel during the scariest moments? How did your body feel?

- -

- -

- -

Have you ever wondered why being scared makes your heart beat faster and makes you breathe quicker? It's actually pretty cool. Your body's reaction to fear is called the "fight or flight" response.[1]

Here's how it works.

Imagine that you're a caveman or a cavewoman from around 100,000 years ago. (Go ahead and beat on your chest if it helps you get into character.) Now imagine that a very hungry saber-toothed tiger drops by your cave for dinner. Wanna know what's on the menu? YOU.

What do you do? Well, there are two choices: 1. Fight. You pick up the nearest club and battle it out with the tiger. Or, 2. Flight. You yell to the tiger, "What's that over there? A hundred pounds of uneaten steak?!", hope he falls for it, and you run.

Today, your body has the same reaction whenever it's faced with fear. To prepare for fight-or-flight, a number of things happen so your body is ready for action or escape.[2] Your heart rate speeds up to get more blood to your muscles and brain. Your lungs take in air faster to give your body more oxygen. Your pupils get larger so you can see better, and your digestive system slows down so you can concentrate on more important things than going to the bathroom.

That's pretty incredible, right? Our bodies get us ready to face our fears without us even realizing it.

DECODE IT!

Compared to humans today, were cavemen taller or shorter than we are?

Have you ever had to face a fear? Had to do anything that made you afraid or nervous? How did you feel? Did you notice any of your body's fight-or-flight responses?

--- --- --- --- --- --- --- --- --- --- --- --- --- --- --- --- --- ---

--- --- --- --- --- --- --- --- --- --- --- --- --- --- --- --- --- ---

--- --- --- --- --- --- --- --- --- --- --- --- --- --- --- --- --- ---

Ananias was in that exact same place—the place you are right before you have to do something you don't want to do because you're afraid.

God told him to help the Jesus-hater Saul, and Ananias was scared. Because Ananias was a Jesus-lover. Based on what he'd heard about Saul, Ananias had some really good reasons to want to run. But instead of running, Ananias told God that he was afraid. Here is God's response:

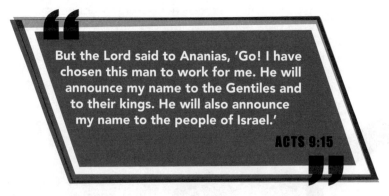

> But the Lord said to Ananias, 'Go! I have chosen this man to work for me. He will announce my name to the Gentiles and to their kings. He will also announce my name to the people of Israel.'
>
> **ACTS 9:15**

God told Ananias to go anyway, even though he was afraid. And do you know what Ananias did?

Ananias went. Ananias obeyed God because he knew that God would be with him.

Listen to this verse from the first chapter of Joshua:

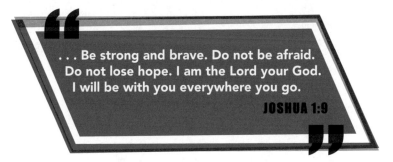

> . . . Be strong and brave. Do not be afraid. Do not lose hope. I am the Lord your God. I will be with you everywhere you go.
>
> **JOSHUA 1:9**

Think back to the fear you wrote before. How do you think that situation would have felt different if you went into it absolutely certain that God was with you?

Part of having faith means trusting that God is with us. Spend a few minutes talking to God. Tell Him that you're thankful He's always with you. Even when it doesn't feel like it. Even when you're afraid.

DAY 3

WHEN YOU'RE AFRAID, YOU CAN TALK TO GOD.

We all have fears. But not everyone is afraid of the same thing. Put the following situations in order from the least scary to the most scary.

Speaking in front of a big crowd
Trying out for a new sport
Someone you love getting sick
Sleeping over at someone's house for the first time
Finding a spider under your blanket
Flying in a hot air balloon
Sitting alone in a dark room
Being the last one picked for a team

LEAST SCARY

MOST SCARY

Now, have someone else in your house put that same list in order from least to most scary. (Give them a sheet of paper to write on, and don't let them see your list before they make their own.)

See? I bet their list was a little different from yours. We all get nervous or afraid sometimes!

One of the best things you can do when you're afraid is to *talk* about it. Studies show that writing or talking about our fears can actually help us overcome them.[3]

When is the last time you remember feeling afraid, nervous, or scared?

_____

_____

_____

_____

Is there something in the future, something that *could* happen, that makes you feel afraid, nervous, or scared?

_____

_____

_____

_____

When God told Ananias to help Saul, Ananias was probably very afraid. But instead of running away or keeping his feelings inside, Ananias talked to God about it. He told God how he was feeling and what he was thinking.

God wants us to do the same thing. An important part of having faith is believing that God hears us when we talk to Him.

Ananias had faith that God heard him when he prayed, and when God told him to go to Saul, Ananias obeyed. Listen to what happened:

> Then Ananias went to the house and entered it. He placed his hands on Saul. 'Brother Saul,' he said, 'you saw the Lord Jesus. He appeared to you on the road as you were coming here. He has sent me so that you will be able to see again. You will be filled with the Holy Spirit.' Right away something like scales fell from Saul's eyes. And he could see again. He got up and was baptized. After eating some food, he got his strength back.
>
> **ACTS 9:17-19**

Because Ananias had faith that God heard him when he prayed, he was able to face his fear.

Find an adult today or tomorrow and show them your responses to the last two questions on page 65. Ask them if they'd be willing to help you face some of your fears by giving you some ideas about how to do that.

BONUS ACTIVITY

Ready to face a fear? The first thing you'll need is someone else to play along. This is very important—*they have to agree to the rules of the game.* If they don't agree, you may end up in a little (or a lot) of trouble!

Grab something that would work as a blindfold. Take turns putting on the blindfold and being spun around a few times. The unblindfolded person will then sneak up behind the blindfolded person and try to scare them.

See who jumps the highest and screams the loudest!

DECODE IT!

What fell from Saul's eyes after Ananias prayed for him?

DAY 4

WHEN YOU'RE AFRAID, YOU CAN REMEMBER GOD'S WORDS.

Let's play a game to test your memory.

What was the name of the first street you lived on?

- -

What was your first pet's name?

- -

Name 3 things you got for Christmas in the past few years.

- -

- -

- -

What color did you wear yesterday?

- -

What's the last song you heard playing?

- -

What's the name of the last restaurant where you ate?

- -

What did you order there? What did everyone else order?

- -

- -

Our brains are what give us the ability to *focus*. And focusing helps us remember things—important things. Our memories are pretty amazing. And for some, our memories are *unbelievable*. Check out the focus these guys had:

- **Kim Peek is said to have memorized every word of every book he'd ever read—over 9,000 books! It took him just 12 seconds to read one page.[4]**
- **In 2017, Zou Lujian memorized an entire deck of cards in just 13.96 seconds.[5]**
- **At just 10 years old, Nischal Narayanam won his first Guinness World Record by memorizing 225 random objects in around twelve minutes.[6]**
- **In 2015, Suresh Kumar Sharma recited the first 70,030 numbers from the number Pi in their correct order. It took him over 7 hours to say them out loud![7]**

Our ability to memorize things makes our brains a pretty powerful tool. And even though we may never set World Records, we can still use our memories to help ourselves and others. We can use our memories to help us face our fears.

For the next activity, you'll need a pair of scissors, a pen or pencil, and a Bible (or Bible app on your device).

On the next page, cut along the dotted lines. You should end up with three rectangles or cards.

Look back at Day 1 where you listed your top three fears. On each card, write down one of the fears you listed. These should be fears you have often. Maybe fear of taking a test. Or fear of being made fun of or laughed at. Or fear of your parents fighting. Whatever your biggest, most frequent fears are: write them down.

Using your Bible, look up each verse listed below. Choose the ones you like most and put a star beside them. Then, decide on your top three and write each one on the back of each fear card.

Joshua 1:9
Psalm 27:1
Isaiah 35:4
Matthew 6:34
John 14:27

Then, carry these cards in your pocket or backpack every day. Whenever you feel that fear creeping in, pull out the card and read the verse on the back. You can even say it out loud. Before long, you'll start to memorize the verses, and you won't need the card anymore. And any time you're nervous or afraid, these verses will begin to pop into your head.

DECODE IT!

Dorothy Straight became the youngest published author in the world at what age?

Look at what happened with Saul when Ananias faced his fear:

> . . . Saul spent several days with the
> believers in Damascus. Right away he
> began to preach in the synagogues. He
> taught that Jesus is the Son of God. All
> who heard him were amazed. They asked,
> 'Isn't he the man who caused great trouble
> in Jerusalem? Didn't he make trouble for
> those who worship Jesus? Hasn't he come
> here to take them as prisoners to the chief
> priests?' But Saul grew more and more
> powerful. The Jews living in Damascus
> couldn't believe what was happening. Saul
> proved to them that Jesus is the Messiah.
>
> **ACTS 9:19-22**

Ananias chose to focus on his faith rather than his fear, and a man's entire life was changed. Because of Saul's faith, others living in Damascus began to have faith, too.

Instead of focusing on your fear, you can choose to focus on God's words. When you face your fears, you can have faith that God is with you, God hears you, and God can do amazing things.

CHALLENGE 3

This week, we've learned a lot about how knowing Jesus can help us face our fears. What's the *main* thing you learned this week that you don't want to forget? (Look back at the bottom lines if you need a reminder!)

- -

- -

Let's test out that amazing memory we talked about last time. Look back and read the definition of faith one time. (Just one time!)

Now, write down as much of the definition as you can remember.

Faith means . . .

- -

- -

Go back to the definition of faith (on page 4) and check your memory. If you need to fill in any missing words, do that now.

Ready for another experiment? This one's a little different. We're going to do an experiment to see how well you can focus and memorize.

The only supplies you need are:
- **A clock or a timer (or the clock or timer on a smartphone or tablet)**
- **A pen or pencil**

Step 1
Set the timer for two minutes.

Step 2
Turn to Table A on page 77.

Step 3
Press START on the timer and study the words in Table A for two minutes, then come back to this page.

Step 4
Now, turn to page 78. Using the blank table, recall as many of the words as you can.

Step 5
How many words were you able to remember? _ _ _ _ _ _ _ _ _

Let's try that again.

Step 1
Set the timer for two minutes.

Step 2
Turn to Table B on page 77.

Step 3
Press START on the timer and study the words in Table B for two minutes, then come back to this page.

Step 4
Now, turn to page 78. Using the blank table, recall as many of the words as you can.

Step 5
How many words were you able to remember? _ _ _ _ _ _ _ _ _

I bet you did better with Table B, didn't you? Look at Table B's
first line of words.

Those words are all _ .

The second line of words are all _ _ _ _ _ _ _ _ _ _ _ _ _ _ _ _ _ _ .

The third line of words are all _ _ _ _ _ _ _ _ _ _ _ _ _ _ _ _ _ _ .

The last line of words are all _ _ _ _ _ _ _ _ _ _ _ _ _ _ _ _ _ _ _ .

Table B's words are easier to memorize because of the *kind of
words* you are memorizing. Table B's words aren't random and
meaningless like Table A's.

The kind of words we focus on matters, especially when we are
feeling nervous, afraid, or scared.

Our bottom line this week is **knowing Jesus can help you
face your fears**. When it comes to facing our fears, words are
a big deal.

> *We can use words to talk to God.*
> *We can use words to talk to adults.*
> *We can read God's words.*

When we focus on words that help us, it's so much easier to face
our fears.

Table A

army	color	fire	table	nine
swing	cell	ring	plugs	lamp
baby	sword	rock	bird	find
hold	desk	horse	clock	worm

Table B

cow	chicken	cat	rabbit	fish
orange	yellow	red	green	purple
apple	grapes	banana	kiwi	mango
teacher	school	math	pencil	class

Table A

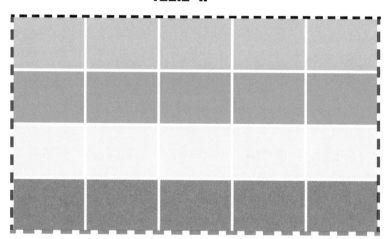

Table B

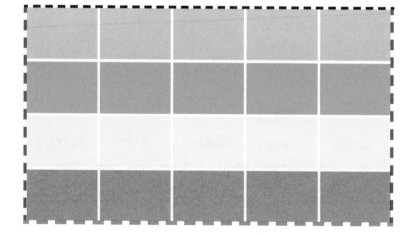

Write a letter to yourself in the space below. Look back at our bottom lines, our Scriptures from Day 4, and our story about Ananias facing his fears and helping Saul. Focus on those words and tell yourself how knowing Jesus can help you face your fears.

ACTS 10

DAY 1

KNOWING JESUS CHANGES THE WAY YOU SEE OTHERS.

Got any colored pencils, crayons, or markers? Grab them and let's get started.

Think back to the last time you met a new person. Maybe it was a kid at the park or your mom's friend from work. How much did you focus on their face and clothes?

Try and remember as much about them as you can by drawing their face, hair, and clothes on the figure to the right.

Did you know that it's good for you to meet new people and make new friends? Interacting with others helps your mind, your heart, and your body. Meeting new people can actually help you live longer![1]

This week let me introduce you to Peter. Peter was a Jesus-follower who became one of Paul's friends. In today's story, Peter meets someone new—a man named Cornelius.

Cornelius was a good guy. He was also a leader in the Roman army. But most importantly, Cornelius loved God. He gave money to people who didn't have enough and he talked to God all the time.

One day, God spoke to Cornelius in a vision—the same way he spoke to Ananias. But this time, God sent an angel to talk to Cornelius. The angel told Cornelius to send for a man named

Peter in a town called Joppa. Cornelius immediately asked a few men who worked for him to go to Joppa to find Peter.

As the men neared Joppa, Peter was climbing up to a rooftop to pray. Then, Peter had a vision, too! But his vision was different from Cornelius'. After his vision, Peter said:

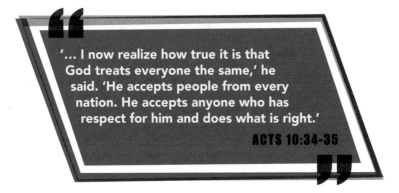

'... I now realize how true it is that God treats everyone the same,' he said. 'He accepts people from every nation. He accepts anyone who has respect for him and does what is right.'

ACTS 10:34-35

What Peter saw would change the rest of history forever. What Peter saw would teach Jesus-followers that the story of Jesus is for everyone—every*one*. Not just the people who look like us, talk like us, or act like us.

Think about someone who is different from you. If you've never met anyone all that different from you, think about someone from YouTube, TV, or a movie.

What makes that person different from you?

1. _

2. _

3. _

4. _

5. _

Now, think really hard.
In what ways are you and this person the same?

1. _

2. _

3. _

4. _

5. _

It's easy to see how people are different from us. Sure, we prefer
different foods, style our hair differently, and enjoy different
hobbies, but in the ways that matter, we're all the same because
we are loved by the one, big God who created us all. Because
of this, we should treat everyone with love and respect.

Meet me back here tomorrow to talk more about how knowing
Jesus changes the way you see others.

DECODE IT!

What was the name of the
city Cornelius' men
found Peter in?

DAY 2

WE CAN TREAT PEOPLE WHO ARE DIFFERENT FROM US WITH LOVE AND RESPECT.

Circle which of the following you like more:

Chocolate or Vanilla

Sports or Games on a Device

Showers or Baths

Hot Weather or Cold Weather

Staying up Late or Going to Bed Early

Top Bunk or Bottom Bunk

Water or Juice

Math or Reading

Breakfast or Dinner

Flying on a Plane or Driving in a Car

BONUS ACTIVITY

Using a different colored pencil or marker, have someone else in your house answer those same questions.

How many of your answers were different? _ _ _ _ _ _ _ _ _ _ _ _

Think about this:

Why can it be hard for us to like or spend time with people who are different from us?

- -

- -

- -

- -

The last time we hung out, we talked about two people who were about to meet for the very first time—Cornelius and Peter. Cornelius and Peter were *very* different from one another.

Cornelius	Peter
Lived in Rome	Traveled all over, tellling people about Jesus
Believed in God	Believed that Jesus is God's son
Non-Jewish	Jewish
Wealthy	Depended on the kindness of others for a home and food

If we made a list of their likes and dislikes, I bet they'd be *very* different from one another. The *one* similarity that both men shared was that they both believed in the one true God—our God.

Remember, an angel appeared in a vision to Cornelius and told him to find Peter in the town of Joppa and invite Peter to his house. To understand why this is such a big deal, you have to understand one *big* difference between Peter and Cornelius; Peter was Jewish, Cornelius was not.

Basically, they were from two different types of cultures. And back then, those two cultures did not hang out together. In fact, Jewish people had a lot of laws that kept non-Jewish people away from them.

Another important difference between Cornelius and Peter was that Cornelius believed in God, but didn't believe that Jesus was God's Son. Peter, on the other hand, had spent a lot of time with Jesus before Jesus died. Peter was even there when Jesus was raised back to life and went to heaven to be with God. Peter had faith that Jesus is God's one and only Son.

Let's get back to their story and see what happens next.

Cornelius' men were close to where Peter was in Joppa, praying on a rooftop. During his prayer, Peter had a vision of a sheet falling from heaven. And on that sheet were a bunch of animals—pigs, rabbits, birds, snakes—all *kinds* of animals. Then a voice spoke to Peter:

...'Get up, Peter. Kill and eat.'

ACTS 10:13

I bet Peter was confused. Jewish law said that it was forbidden to eat those animals. His entire life, Peter had been told that eating them was "unclean" or unacceptable.

Here's what happend next:

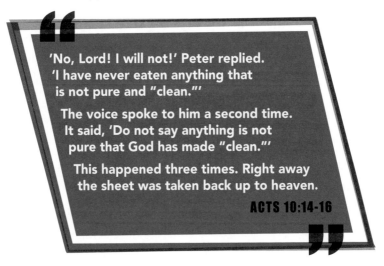

> 'No, Lord! I will not!' Peter replied. 'I have never eaten anything that is not pure and "clean."'
>
> The voice spoke to him a second time. It said, 'Do not say anything is not pure that God has made "clean."'
>
> This happened three times. Right away the sheet was taken back up to heaven.
>
> **ACTS 10:14-16**

Peter was wondering what the vision meant when Cornelius' men showed up asking for him. God spoke to Peter and told him to go wherever the men wanted. So, Peter went downstairs and said, "I'm the one you're looking for."

The men told Peter that Cornelius had invited Peter to visit his home. And even though Peter was Jewish and Cornelius wasn't, Peter agreed to go.

When Peter met Cornelius, he told Cornelius about his vision. And by then, Peter had figured out what it meant: No one was unclean in the eyes of God.

To be "unclean" was like being less-than, looked down on, or left out. And God gave Peter the vision of the animals to say that *no one* was unclean if God said they were clean. And according to God, each and every person on the planet was made clean because they were created by God.

God sent Jesus for the Jewish people and the non-Jewish people. And because of that, God wanted Peter to love Cornelius and other non-Jews the same way he loved Jews. He wanted Peter to tell *everyone* about Jesus.

God wants the same thing from us. He wants us to treat everyone with love and respect.

Think about someone who is different from you. Maybe it's someone at school who eats lunch alone. Or the kid on your soccer team who talks too much. Or maybe someone on your bus, at your church, or even your sibling.

Now, think about three ways you can show that person love and respect:

1. _____

_____

2. _____

_____

3. _____

_____

BONUS ACTIVITY

Choose one of your answers and make it happen this week!

DECODE IT!

In Peter's vision, how many times did he see the sheet fall from heaven?

DAY 3

WE CAN TREAT OUR FAMILY WITH LOVE AND RESPECT.

List the names of the people who live with you.

- -

- -

- -

- -

- -

- -

Thinking about the last few weeks, who on this list did you . . .

Talk back to?

Argue with?

Tell on?

Get angry at?

Raise your voice to?

If your family is like most families, you could probably answer with anyone's name to any of those questions.

In your life, your family are the people you will spend the most time with. They're also the people who can make us the maddest, saddest, or the most frustrated.

Maybe that's why we often treat our friends and teachers with more love and respect than we do the people in our family.

What do you think? Why is it easier to be kind to our best friend than it is to be kind to our siblings? Why do you think we obey our teachers right away when our parents have to beg us to do our chores?

Reread this verse from Day 1:

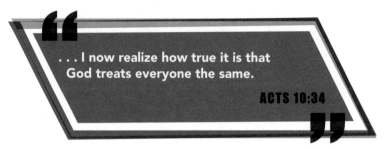

> . . . I now realize how true it is that
> God treats everyone the same.
>
> ACTS 10:34

Underline the word *everyone*. God wants us to treat our families with the same love and respect that we treat our friends with.

The problem is that our focus is off. But it's not really our fault. Let me explain. When we see our friends, the part of our brain in charge of serotonin is activated.[2] Serotonin is a chemical that makes us feel happy and relaxed. On the other hand, that doesn't always happen when we see our families.

But what if we switched our focus? We can't rewire our brains, but we can rewire our actions.

For example, instead of coming home and demanding a snack before disappearing into your room, you can ask your parents about their day and offer to watch your little brother while Dad makes dinner.

Your turn. Fill in the blanks below with ways you can treat your family with the same love and respect that you show your friends and teachers.

Instead of putting off chores until Mom/Dad is super frustrated, I can

- -

Instead of yelling at my sibling when they're being annoying, I can

- -

Instead of complaining about what I'm eating for dinner, I can

- -

Instead of pointing out what my parents *don't* do for me, I can

- -

Instead of reacting with anger when I don't get my way, I can

- -

It's not always going to be easy, and you're not going to get it right all the time, but treating your family with love and respect will change your entire home for the better.

Spend a few minutes talking to God. Ask Him to help you focus on His words and to help you treat *everyone* with love and respect.

DAY 4

WE CAN TREAT EVERYONE WITH LOVE AND RESPECT . . . EVEN WHEN IT'S HARD.

Has there been a time when someone hurt your feelings? Maybe . . .

- **A friend didn't invite you to their party.**
- **The coach didn't put you in the entire game.**
- **Your punishment was worse than your little brother's.**

Write about a time you felt hurt or sad because of something someone else did:

- -

- -

- -

- -

- -

- -

The thing about hurt feelings is that they hurt. Sometimes, they hurt a lot. Maybe you cry when your feelings are hurt. Or you get angry and want to punch a wall. (I don't recommend this. Pillows are better things to punch.) But regardless of how you react on the outside, on the inside, it just *hurts*.

Did you know that our brains can confuse emotional pain with physical pain?[3] When our minds process our hurt feelings, it affects the same area of the brain that tells us when we're in physical pain.

When we're hurt by someone, it's especially hard to be kind to them. Maybe you don't have any real enemies, but you can probably name a few people who have hurt you or upset you.

Did you know that God wants us to be kind to those people, too? He does. That doesn't mean you have to be best friends with someone who has hurt your feelings over and over again, but it does mean that we should show everyone love and respect—even people we don't like.

Which brings us back to the story of Cornelius and Peter.

After meeting Cornelius and telling him about his vision, Peter walked with Cornelius into a large room filled with people. And not just *any* people—these were all non-Jews. Peter was breaking a very serious Jewish law by entering the home of a person who was not Jewish, but he didn't care. He didn't care because the vision showed him that the story of Jesus was for everyone—that anyone created by God was to be treated with love and respect.

And everyone means . . . everyone.

And then Peter began telling non-Jewish people about Jesus. Remember, these people believed in God, but hadn't yet believed that Jesus is God's Son. Before his vision, Peter would have never shared the Good News of Jesus with people who weren't Jewish. They were considered "outsiders" and "unclean." But on this day, he had a message for them:

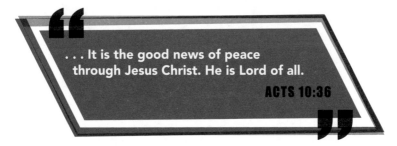

> . . . It is the good news of peace through Jesus Christ. He is Lord of all.
>
> **ACTS 10:36**

God showed Peter that knowing Jesus changes the way we treat other people—even people we don't like.

And because Peter showed love and respect to Cornelius and his friends and family, they heard the story of Jesus and they all became believers. Their lives were changed *forever.*

So, how can you show love and respect to someone who has hurt you or upset you? How can you show love and respect to someone you don't really like?

You can . . .

- **forgive them.**
- **pray for them.**
- **pray for your attitude toward them.**
- **refrain from saying bad things about them.**
- **ask your friends not to put them down.**

Your turn to think of an idea. What is one way you can treat someone you don't like with love and respect?

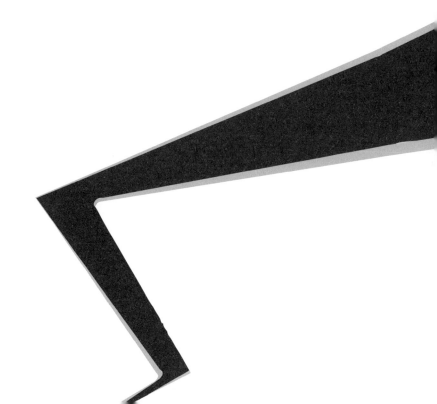

CHALLENGE 4

This week, we've learned a lot of things about how knowing
Jesus changes the way you see others. What's the *main* thing
you learned this week that you don't want to forget? (Look back
at the bottom lines if you need a reminder!)

-- --

-- --

-- --

-- --

I hope you were really *focused* this week, because a lot
happened in our story! Let's review together. Number the
paragraphs on the next page 1 through 6 in the order that
they happened.

I'll wait right here while you're doing that . . .

. . .

Done?

How'd you do? Did you have to look back in the sessions
to remember the correct order? Remember—your *focus* is
important!

Now, turn the page for more!

And then Peter began telling the non-Jewish people about Jesus. Remember, these people believed in God, but hadn't yet believed that Jesus is God's Son. Before his vision, Peter would have never shared the Good News of Jesus with them. They were considered "outsiders" and "unclean." But on this day, he had a message for them: ". . . It is the good news of peace through Jesus Christ. He is Lord of all."

As the men neared Joppa, Peter was climbing up to a rooftop to pray. During his prayer, Peter had a vision of a sheet falling from heaven. And on that sheet were a bunch of animals—pigs, rabbits, birds, snakes—all kinds of animals. Then a voice spoke to Peter: ". . .'Get up, Peter. Kill and eat.'"

One day, God spoke to Cornelius in a vision—the same way he spoke to Ananias. But this time, God sent an angel to talk to Cornelius. The angel told Cornelius to send for a man named Peter in a town called Joppa. Cornelius immediately asked a few men who worked for him to go to Joppa to find Peter.

Because Peter showed love and respect to Cornelius and his friends and family, they heard the story of Jesus and they all became believers. Their lives were changed forever.

After meeting Cornelius and telling him about his vision, Peter and Cornelius walked together into a large room filled with people. And not just any people—these were non-Jewish people. Peter was breaking a very serious Jewish law by entering the home of a non-Jewish person, but he didn't care. He didn't care because the vision he'd seen showed him that the story of Jesus was for everyone.

Peter was wondering what the vision meant when Cornelius' men showed up asking for him. God spoke to Peter and told him to go wherever the men wanted. So, Peter went downstairs and said, "I'm the one you're looking for." The men told Peter that Cornelius had invited Peter to visit his home. And even though Peter was Jewish and Cornelius wasn't, Peter agreed to go.

I have some good news and some bad news. The bad news is that there is no experiment this week. The good news is that we're going to do something equally as cool.

The only supplies you need are:

- **A device with Internet access**
- **Permission from an adult at home to use it**

Step 1
Go to www.Google.com/maps

Step 2
Enter your home address

Step 3
Click the square that says "Satellite View"

Pretty crazy, right?
You should be able to see exactly where you live.

Step 4

Now, zoom out until you can see another house or building. You may see a bunch of houses. If you do, close your eyes and randomly point to one on your computer screen.

Step 5
In the space below, name the home. You can name it based off the street name, the color of the house, a weird tree in the front yard. It doesn't matter what you name it—just be creative!

The _ **house.**

Step 6

Tonight, before you go to sleep, pray for whoever lives there. It doesn't matter who they are, what they like or dislike, or even what they believe.

BONUS STEP

Complete this exercise a couple of times in the next few weeks. Ask your family to pray, too.

Our bottom line this week is **knowing Jesus changes the way you see others.** He wants us to treat everyone with love and respect—people who are different from us, our families, people who have hurt us—everyone.

After you pray for the people in the house you chose, ask God to help you see them the way *He* sees them.

DECODE IT!

People who have photographic memories can recall information they've read only one time. What is this type of memory called?

WEEK 5
GRACE IS A GIFT

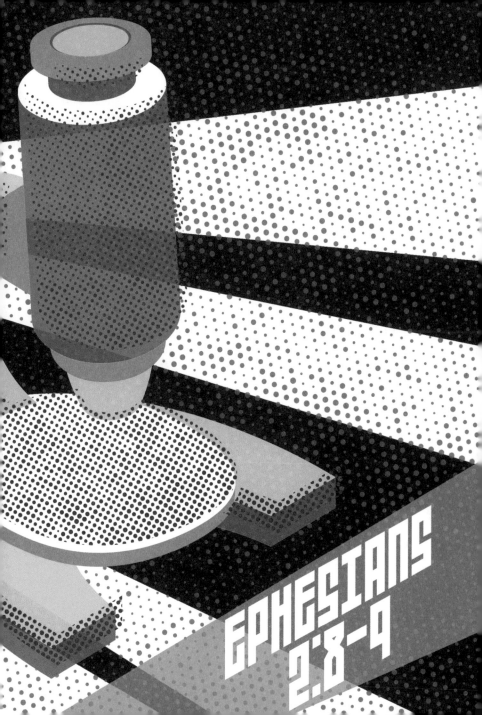

DAY 1

JESUS IS A GIFT FOR EVERYONE.

We live during a pretty amazing time. We're surrounded by all sorts of technology that wasn't around when our parents and grandparents were our age.

And science isn't finished yet! Check out these amazing technologies that are being developed right now:

- **Hyperloop** – This train-like vehicle will travel through tubes at a speed of 600 miles per hour. That means a trip from San Francisco to Los Angeles (which normally takes six hours) would only take around 35 minutes!

- **GeeFi** – This device will give you access to unlimited wi-fi anywhere in the world.

- **Wireless electricity** – By putting a magnetic field in the air, any device that's brought near it will automatically have power without having to plug it in.

- **Self-driving cars** – Cars that drive themselves will make traffic better and lessen the number of car accidents that happen. Plus, how cool would it be to have family movie night while you're on a road trip?

- **Helium balloon rides to space** – By taking a special capsule attached to a helium balloon, you may be able to take a ride up to space . . . for the low, low price of $124,000![1]

Those all sound amazing, right? Some of them even sound too good to be true.

That's something we're going to talk about this week—something that sounds too good to be true . . . but *is* true. And that thing is *grace*. No, not your classmate named Grace. We're talking about the word—not the name. So what does "grace" mean?

Let's start with what Paul says about grace:

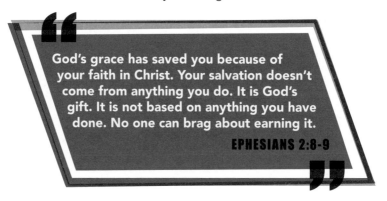

> God's grace has saved you because of your faith in Christ. Your salvation doesn't come from anything you do. It is God's gift. It is not based on anything you have done. No one can brag about earning it.
>
> **EPHESIANS 2:8-9**

We learn a *lot* about grace in those verses.

1. **Graces saves us.**

2. **Grace doesn't come from anything we do.**
   No one can earn grace.

3. **We learn that grace is a gift.**
   It's the gift of forgiveness every time we mess up.
   It's the gift of being loved by God
   before we even know who He is.
   It's the gift of being in God's family forever,
   no matter what.

Grace is the best kind of gift, because it's given to *everyone.* No one is excluded from it. *Jesus* is a gift for everyone. (Sound familiar?!)

More on that later. For now, know that grace sounds too good to be true, but it *is* true. It's real. Because God gives it to us.

Let's go back to that list of inventions. Which of those sounds the *most* too good to be true? Which would you enjoy the most and why?

_ _

_ _

_ _

_ _

DECODE IT!

Which American inventor has the most inventions credited to him?

DAY 2

WE CAN'T EARN GRACE.

Have you ever had a slap bracelet? You know, those bracelets that look like sticks with rounded ends until you slap them on your wrist and they become a bracelet? Ever wondered who invented them? (Probably not, but you're about to find out anyway!)

In 1983, high school teacher Stuart Anders came up with the idea of slap bracelets when he was playing with steel ribbon in his father's shop. By 1990, orders for slap bracelets were so large that they stopped counting the number of bracelets sold and started counting them by the pounds of bracelets sold. Then, in 2013, Apple, inc. filed a patent to use the same kind of material Mr. Anders used in his slap bracelets.

One day, Stuart is a teacher hanging out in his dad's garage, and then, he's a millionaire who owns technology being bought by Apple!

Isn't that incredible? It sounds too good to be true, but it *is* true. It happened!

So, what do you want to be when you grow up? A millionaire like Stuart Anders? Maybe. But how are you going to earn money? Even if it's not millions of dollars? People earn money in all kinds of fun and unique ways.

On each line below, circle which job you'd prefer to have more:

Zoo Keeper	**OR**	*Video Game Creator*
Shoe Designer	**OR**	*Illustrator*
Professional Athlete	**OR**	*Actor*
Amusement Park Test Rider	**OR**	*Dessert Taste Tester*
Restaurant Manager	**OR**	*Ballpark Manager*
Toy Designer	**OR**	*Skateboard Instructor*
Stunt Person	**OR**	*Professional Storyteller*
Musician	**OR**	*Firefighter*

From the time we're able to talk, we're taught that we need to work in order to earn things. It's no wonder that grace (which is completely free) is hard for us to understand.

We can pray for forgiveness and get forgiven *every time*?

God will love us no matter what we do *forever*?

You can work really hard and earn money, respect, even fame. But you can't earn grace. Grace is something you are given—for free—every minute of every day. Let's look at our verses for the week again:

> **God's grace has saved you because of your faith in Christ. Your salvation doesn't come from anything you do. It is God's gift. It is not based on anything you have done. No one can brag about earning it.**
>
> **EPHESIANS 2:8-9**

Underline the second-to-last sentence: *It is not based on anything you have done.*

Grace is a gift given to us. We can't do anything to earn it or deserve it. All it takes to receive grace is to believe that Jesus is God's Son. All it takes to receive grace is to have faith.

Spend a few minutes talking to God, telling Him how thankful you are for His free gift of grace.

DAY 3

WE CAN GIVE GRACE TO OTHERS.

Most inventions are created as a solution to a problem. In other words, they make our lives easier. Think about spending one day without these inventions:

- **Cars**
- **Electricity**
- **The Internet**
- **Computers**
- **Cell phones**

Out of all those inventions, which would be the hardest to live without? Why?

- -

- -

- -

- -

You know what else would be really hard to live without? Forgiveness. We wouldn't have relationships with . . . *anyone.*

Your mom would have never spoken to you again after that slime-on-the-new-rug incident.

Your best friend would have become your worst enemy after you forgot to invite him to the new Marvel movie. Your teacher would refuse to call on you after you snuck your phone into class.

But sometimes, living without forgiveness seems like the easier option, right? Forgiving someone when they've hurt you or made you upset is really hard. When . . .

**your friend tells you a lie,
your parents break a promise,
or your sibling blames their mess on you,**

. . . you are mad. You are hurt. And you have every right to feel that way. But you don't have a right to stay that way.

Look back to our verses:

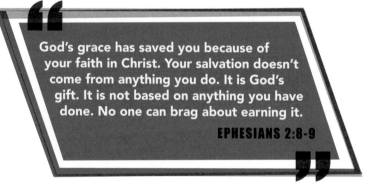

God's grace has saved you because of your faith in Christ. Your salvation doesn't come from anything you do. It is God's gift. It is not based on anything you have done. No one can brag about earning it.

EPHESIANS 2:8-9

Underline the sentence *It is God's gift.*

Because of grace, any time we ask for forgiveness, God gives us forgiveness. It's like whatever we did never even happened. He fully forgives—right then and there. Because of that, God wants us to forgive others when they mess up. Even when it's really, really hard.

How do we do that? How do we forgive when we don't want to forgive?

1. **Ask for God's help.**
2. **Read God's Word.**
3. **Talk to an adult you trust and tell them how you're feeling.**

Think of someone who has hurt your feelings or made you upset. In the space below, write that person a note. Tell them everything you're feeling. Tell them that they hurt you or that they made you angry. Then, on the last line, write down these words:

Because of the grace God has given me,
I want to give you grace, too. I forgive you.

- -

- -

- -

- -

- -

- -

- -

- -

- -

- -

- -

- -

You may not feel "okay" around that person right away. That's okay. Sometimes we have to keep forgiving someone over and over again before we feel it in our hearts.

Keep talking to God about it. And keep saying or writing down these words until they feel true:

> **But because of the grace God has given me,**
> **I want to give (Person's Name) grace, too.**
> **I forgive (Person's Name).**

DAY 4

FAITH IS THE ONLY REQUIREMENT FOR GRACE.

Before we get started, grab a pen or pencil.

Check all of the following that you have used before:

☐ Telescope
☐ Sunglasses
☐ Contact lenses
☐ Eyeglasses
☐ Magnifying glass
☐ Microscope
☐ X-ray machine
☐ Camera
☐ Camera lenses

Have you ever thought about all the inventions that exist to help us see better?

A long time ago, like three *thousand* years ago, in 1000 BC (before Jesus was even born!), the first invention to help people see better was born. It was called a reading stone, a glass ball that was laid on top of writing to make it larger and easier to read.[2]

Now, a couple thousand years later, we have something called eSight Glasses®. eSight uses a high definition camera and a bunch of other cool technology to help people who are blind to see.[3]

Can you imagine? Not really knowing what your own face looks like, then sliding on a pair of $10,000 glasses and being able to see it for the first time?

We've come a long way in a thousand years.

You know who could have used some eSight Glasses®? Saul! Remember? He was *totally blind* for three days after meeting Jesus on the road to Damascus. Think about how scared he must have been, not knowing if he'd ever be able to see again.

We've said that faith is trusting in what you can't see because of what you can see. For Saul, he knew his vision was gone, but he also knew that Jesus had appeared to him and spoken to him. The Bible doesn't tell us whether or not Saul was afraid, but we do know that Saul obeyed Jesus and went into the city to wait to hear what to do next.

This was Saul's first act of faith.

DECODE IT!

In which country is the most powerful digital camera in the world located?

How about you? Have you ever done something just because of your faith in God? How strong do you think your faith is now?

Look at the circle to the right. In the center of the circle is a dot. The center of the circle represents a very strong faith—you have prayed to invite Jesus into your heart and life, you talk to God most days, and you read the Bible most days, too. The outside of the circle is as far away from strong faith as you can get. You never talk to God and you never read the Bible. (HINT: If you're reading this book, you're not on the outside of the circle!)

Think about your faith. Mark an X somewhere inside the circle. The closer the X is to the center of the circle, the stronger you think your faith is right now.

Now, draw a star inside the circle to represent where you want your faith to be.

If you're not as close to the center as you want to be, that's okay. That's most people! Your faith will continue to grow and change, as you grow and change.

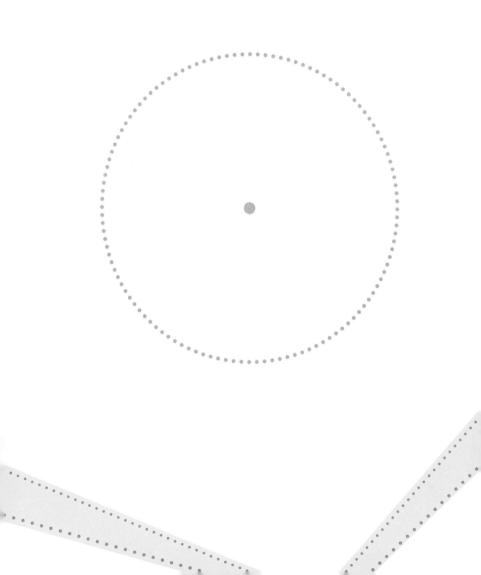

Now let's look back to our verses for the week.

> **God's grace has saved you because of your faith in Christ. Your salvation doesn't come from anything you do. It is God's gift. It is not based on anything you have done. No one can brag about earning it.**
>
> **EPHESIANS 2:8-9**

Underline the first sentence: *God's grace has saved you because of your faith in Christ.* Then, circle the words *your faith in Christ.*

The only requirement to receive God's free gift of grace is faith. That's all we need—to be able to trust in what we can't see because of what we can see.

If you've never invited Jesus into your life and heart, but you feel like you might be ready for that, turn to page 196 to learn more.

If you're not ready to take that step, that's okay. Keep reading this book and learning more!

And finally, for those of you who have already taken that step, there are many ways to grow stronger in your faith.

1. **Hear: Listen to God's Words**
   When we read the Bible, and listen to what God has to tell us through His word, we learn we can Trust God no matter what.
2. **Pray: Dialogue with God**
   Through prayer we connect with God. We show gratitude for who He is and what He's done. Through prayer, we can be honest with saying we're sorry for what we've done and expressing how we're feeling about what's happening in our lives.
3. **Talk: Articulate Your Faith**
   When we talk about faith with other people who also have a relationship with God, we can see God. Talking about your faith is a great way to discuss and examine God's word with others who also know God. We can also share our faith with those who don't yet have a relationship with Jesus.
4. **Live: Worship with Your Life**
   Worshipping God is more than just singing songs. Worshipping is about living life in a way that honors God.

These are just a few ideas that can help move you from where you are in your faith to where you want to be.

CHALLENGE 5

This week, we've learned that Jesus is a gift for everyone. What's the *main* thing you learned this week that you don't want to forget? (Look back at the bottom lines if you need a reminder!)

- -

- -

Let's do a quick review to check how focused you were this week. If you need to look back to check your answers, do it!

Ephesians 2:8-9 tells us that grace is a _ _ _ _ _ _ _ _ _ _ _ _ _ _ .

You can't _ grace.

God wants us to _ _ _ _ _ _ _ _ _ _ others when they mess up.

_ _ _ _ _ _ _ _ _ _ _ _ _ _ is the only requirement for grace.

How'd you do?
Ready for a little fun?

We've talked a lot about inventions. One reason inventions are so fascinating is that they usually use never-before-seen technology to help people live their lives.

In today's experiment, you're going to become an inventor. That's right! YOU are going to dream up an idea that sounds too good to be true.

Supplies needed:

- **Colored pencils, crayons, or markers**
- **Pen or pencil**

Step 1
Define the problem.

What is a problem you or other people face every day that you'd like to help solve?

- -

- -

Step 2
What are a few ideas you can think of that may help solve this problem?

1. -

- -

2. -

- -

3. -

- -

Step 3

Now, pretend you have no obstacles. You have all the money in the world, all the technology in the world, and all the help in the world. Looking at your answers from before, what is something you could invent to solve the problem? Describe how your invention would help people:

- -

- -

- -

- -

- -

- -

Step 4

Now, name your invention.

- -

- -

Step 5

In the space provided, draw your invention.

Step 6

What will life be like for people after they use your invention?

_ _

_ _

_ _

_ _

BONUS STEP

Create a model of your invention. You can use a shoe box and craft supplies. You can use playdough or modeling clay. You could also bake a cake (with an adult's help and permission!) and use icing and candy to represent the different parts of your invention.

DECODE IT!

In April 2008, Sam Houghton became the youngest inventor to receive a patent for his "Sweeping Device with Two Hands." How old was he?

Our bottom line this week is **Jesus is a gift for everyone.** If you think about it, God's creation of grace really is the greatest invention of all time.

1. **There was a problem.** Our sins—the stuff we do that's wrong—keep us away from God.

2. **God came up with a solution.** God sent us Jesus. Jesus came to Earth. He lived a perfect life, died, and came back to life to prove that He is God's Son.

3. **We can be forgiven.** Through our faith in Jesus, we can be in God's family forever. We can ask forgiveness for our sins, and we can be forgiven. Every time. No matter what.

Spend a few minutes thanking God for His gift to us.

WEEK 6
PAUL IN ATHENS

ACTS 17:16-34

DAY 1

YOU CAN HELP OTHERS KNOW JESUS.

NOTE: *Tell a parent that you're going to need a magnet by the end of the week. You may already have one in your house. If you don't, you'll need it for some pretty cool experiments on Challenge Day!*

Have you ever had a set of magnets? Maybe they were the letters of the alphabet that you stuck to the fridge. Or maybe you had a fancy magnet kit that you learned how to do tricks or experiments with.

Magnets are one of the oldest forms of technology that exist. It may sound weird to call magnetics technology, but that's what they are.

Check out these cool facts about magnets. I think some of them will surprise you!

- **Volcanoes helped form the first-discovered magnetic stones called magnetite.**
- **Compasses work by a magnetic pull toward the Earth's opposite poles.**
- **The Earth and its poles are like one big magnet.**
- **The most powerful magnets in the universe are stars called magnetars.**
- **Magnets always have two poles (opposite sides)—even if you cut them in half.**[1]

Magnetism is caused by the motion of electric charges.[2] If you've ever used a magnet, you know that they can attract things. Sometimes, the pull is so strong that the object can't resist moving toward the magnet.

Remember our buddy, Paul? (And don't forget: Paul = Saul.) After meeting Jesus and becoming a Jesus-follower, Paul's entire life changed, and Paul became something like a magnet himself—a magnet drawing people closer to Jesus. After meeting Jesus and realizing that Jesus is God's Son, Paul traveled everywhere he could to share his faith, moving people closer and closer to a faith of their own.

One of the towns Paul visited was Athens. And something bad was going on there. Here's what happened:

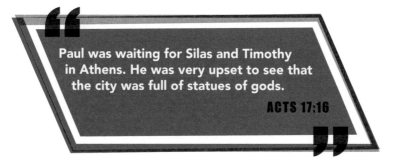

Paul was waiting for Silas and Timothy in Athens. He was very upset to see that the city was full of statues of gods.

ACTS 17:16

The people of Athens were worshipping statues and not the one true God. The people of Athens were very, very far from having faith. They did not believe that Jesus is God's Son. So, Paul decided to do something about it. He decided to draw the people closer to a real faith of their own. Just like a Jesus-magnet.

That's what we're going to talk about this week: how you can be a Jesus-magnet, too. There are lots of ways to be a Jesus-magnet, to draw others closer to Jesus. You can . . .

Show kindness
Pray for people
Pray with people
Forgive
Tell people about Jesus
Invite someone to church
Give someone this book

God wants you to tell others about Him—to be a Jesus-magnet. Part of growing a stronger faith means sharing that faith with the people around you.

Start by making a list of people you see regularly—every day or almost every day. These can be people who already have faith, people who don't have faith, and people whose faith you're not sure about. Just write down the first few people who come to mind:

1. _____

2. _____

3. _____

4. _____

5. _____

6. _____

7. _

8. _

9. _

10. _

Choose one name from that list. Take a few minutes and ask
God how you can be a Jesus-magnet for that person, drawing
them closer and closer to a stronger faith.

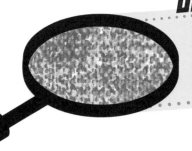

DECODE IT!

**What city from today's story
is Europe's oldest capital
and also one of the oldest
cities in the world?**

DAY 2

YOU HAVE WHAT IT TAKES TO TELL OTHERS ABOUT JESUS.

Below is an image that should be pretty familiar to you. It's the best planet of them all—planet Earth. Looking at it, put a star beside where you are right now. (You don't have to be exact, but at least get the country right!)

Did you know that the Earth acts like one big magnet? It's surrounded by a magnetic field that extends nearly 60,000km into space.[3] That's seriously far!

Here's a way to picture a magnetic field. If you put a magnet onto a table and place an iron nail nearby, what do you think will happen? If you push the magnet toward the nail, there will be a point where the nail jumps across and sticks to the magnet. That's because magnets have an invisible magnetic field that surrounds them.[4]

You've heard of the North Pole, right? Well, there's also a South Pole. Go ahead and label those on the image below.

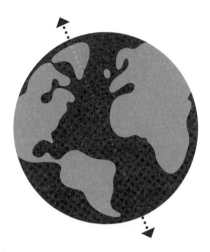

The north end of a magnet points toward the North Pole and the south end of a magnet points toward the South Pole. That's how magnetic compasses work.

Isn't that cool? The Earth has its very own magnetic technology that helps people find their way.

This may sound a little weird, but God wants us to help people find their way, too. He wants us to help people find their way . . . to *Him*.

That's exactly what Paul did when he visited Athens. He saw that the people there were lost. Not like that time you got lost in the grocery store and couldn't find your dad, but lost as in their hearts were lost. They weren't following the one true God.

Listen to what happened:

> So he went to the synagogue. There he talked both with Jews and with Greeks who worshiped God. Each day he spoke with anyone who happened to be in the market place. A group of Epicurean and Stoic thinkers began to argue with him. Some of them asked, 'What is this fellow chattering about?' Others said, 'He seems to be telling us about gods we've never heard of.' They said this because Paul was preaching the good news about Jesus. He was telling them that Jesus had risen from the dead.
>
> **ACTS 17:17-18**

Paul was upset that the people in Athens didn't know Jesus. He went and talked to anyone who would listen to him and he told them the Good News of Jesus.

And that's what God wants you to do.

Maybe you don't feel like you have what it takes to tell others about Jesus. Maybe you're not even sure what you think about Jesus yet. That's okay. The truth is, you've learned a lot already just by reading this book! You may feel like you don't know everything, but you can tell your friends what you *do* know. You have what it takes to tell others about Jesus.

All it takes is your willingness to be brave and bold and make the first step.

Paul didn't know Jesus as well as Jesus' friends did. But that didn't stop him from telling what he *did* know. Paul was brave and bold. Paul took the first step.

If you want to help people find their way to Jesus, you have to take the first step. Here are a few examples of first steps you could take. Finish out the list with some ideas of your own:

- **Invite a friend to church.**
- **Tell a friend who is going through a hard time that you're praying for them (then, *actually* pray for them).**
- **Give your friend a copy of this book.**

It doesn't matter how old you are, how far along you are in your faith, or how much of the Bible you've read—all you need to tell others about Jesus is the willingness to take the first step.

Choose one of the options from the list above and make it happen. Take that first step! And remember—not only do you have what it takes to tell others about Jesus, but He will be with you every step of the way.

DECODE IT!

You're standing on which pole if everywhere you're looking is South?

DAY 3

YOU CAN TELL OTHERS ABOUT JESUS THROUGH YOUR ACTIONS.

Let's check in on your focus. What are two things you've learned about magnets so far this week?

1. _

2. _

We've talked a lot about magnets the last couple of days, but we haven't really broken down what makes a magnet a magnet.

This is going to get science-y for just a minute. Stick with me!

From your skin, to your tablet, to your backpack, to the last slice of pizza you ate, all matter is made up of tiny particles called atoms. Atoms have something called electrons spinning all around them. Most of the time, their electrons spin around like crazy in random directions. But sometimes, they all decide to work together and spin in the same direction. When that happens, voilà! You have magnetism.[5]

Magnetism really isn't that complicated, is it? It's actually pretty simple. And it only takes *one thing* to make it work.

If we want to learn how to be Jesus-magnets—people who draw others closer to Jesus—there's one thing we can do to pull people toward a stronger faith. There is one thing we can do that will make people want to hear what we have to say. We can do one thing that will show people we know the one true God.

Ready to hear what that one thing is?

We can *be kind*.

See? That's not complicated, either.

Think about it. When is the last time someone was nice to you for no reason? Someone . . .

. . . shared their snack with you.
. . . helped you with your homework.
. . . moved seats so you could sit by your friend.
. . . gave you a compliment.

When was the last time someone showed you kindness?

- -

- -

- -

- -

When people are kind to us, we remember it. We remember *them*. People who are kind for no reason are different—they're noticeable. They stand out. We're drawn to kind people because they're easy to be around.

Being kind will always pull people closer to you and closer to Jesus.

When Paul went to Athens, he was upset by what they were doing—worshiping false gods statues instead of the one true God. Instead of telling them that they were dumb or wrong, Paul started off by complimenting them.

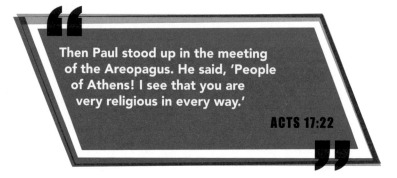

Then Paul stood up in the meeting of the Areopagus. He said, 'People of Athens! I see that you are very religious in every way.'

ACTS 17:22

Then, he told them he had "carefully" looked at the things they were worshipping. He told them that instead of worshipping "an unknown God," they could be worshipping the "God who made the world."

If Paul had walked into Athens and screamed his head off, do you think the people would have been willing to listen to him? No. Instead, he was kind. He gently and simply showed the people of Athens the better way—Jesus.

Helping people understand who is Jesus doesn't have to be complicated. You can start by being kind to others.

Copy your list from Day 1 below. Beside each person's name, write down one way you can show them kindness.

DAY 4

YOU CAN TELL OTHERS ABOUT JESUS WITH YOUR WORDS.

On Day 1 you read some pretty awesome facts about magnets. One of those was that the strongest magnets in the universe are actually stars. Let's see how focused you were . . . do you remember what those types of stars are called?

(No peeking!)

- -

Okay, if you have to flip back, that's cool. Do that now and then fill in the blank.

A magnetar has a magnetic field as strong as around 1,000,000,000,000,000 Gauss.[6] (A Gauss is just the way we measure magnetism—kind of like pounds for weight or miles for distance.) Do you see all those zeroes? That's a lot, a *lot*, of magnetic power.

To give you a little perspective, here are some comparisons:

- **Earth's magnetic field = 0.6 Gauss**
- **A common magnet (like one on your fridge) = 100 Gauss**
- **Sunspots (the most magnetic parts of the Sun) = ~3,000 Gauss**
- **MRI machines (used by doctors to take pictures of the inside of your body) = Up to 70,000 Gauss**

- **Highly magnetized white dwarf stars =
  Up to 1 billion Gauss**
- **Typical neutron stars = ~1 trillion Gauss**

In other words, a magnetar has a magnetic field that is around 100 -1,000 times more magnetically powerful than the next most powerful thing. They're a billion times more magnetic than anything humans can produce in labs, and trillions of times more magnetic than sunspots. In 1/5th of a second, a magnetar can give off as much energy as the Sun would in 250,000 years.[7]

Crazy, right? Don't worry—magnetars aren't close enough to Earth for us to notice, but just reading how powerful magnetars are is kind of scary.

Magnetars have a giant, incredible, irresistible pull. And after Paul started following Jesus, *he* had a giant, incredible, irresistible pull.

What does that mean? That means people followed Paul. They believed what he said. When he told others about Jesus, they listened.

Have you ever met someone with a giant, incredible, irresistible pull? Someone you couldn't help but want to be around? Someone you couldn't help but like? Someone you couldn't help but want to be like? List a few of their characteristics (words that describe them) below:

1. _____

2. _____

3. _____

You may not have listed this word, but usually people like this are described as *confident*. Do you know what that words means? If you don't, use your favorite device to look it up or ask an adult.

In your own words, what does it mean to be confident?

_____

_____

When Paul saw that the people in Athens were worshipping gods that weren't the one true God, he respectfully told them they were wrong. Then, he told them about Jesus. He told them not knowing how they would respond. Here's what happened:

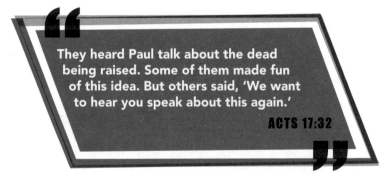

> They heard Paul talk about the dead being raised. Some of them made fun of this idea. But others said, 'We want to hear you speak about this again.'
> **ACTS 17:32**

Some of the people Paul told about Jesus believed him and wanted to hear more. But some of them made fun of Paul. Do you know what Paul did? He kept right on telling people that Jesus was God's Son. He didn't slow down. He didn't get his feelings hurt. He didn't even get mad at the people who made fun of him. He kept right on, confidently telling people about his faith.

And because he did, countless people came to know the story of Jesus.

God wants us to do that, too. He wants us to tell others about Him. He wants us to share our faith by sharing what we know about Him. And sometimes, we need to share our faith with people by talking about Him. You can tell others about Jesus with your words.

You can't control how a person will respond. They may make fun of you, just like some of the people in Athens made fun of Paul. But be confident—just as Paul was confident. Because there are so many people who need to hear the story of Jesus. And you never know—you may be the reason someone begins a faith of their own!

It might be hard to know where to start when you're telling someone the story of Jesus. Brainstorm a few ideas on how you could start that conversation. There are a few examples below to get you started:

- *"What do you do on the weekends? Most Sundays, my family and I go to church and my Small Group Leader is hilarious. Last week, we learned a story from the Bible. Want to hear it?"*
- *"I went through a really hard time once. Something that really helped was talking to God. Do you ever talk to God?"*
- *"Sometimes I get really angry and the only thing that makes me feel better is remembering God's words. I read them in the Bible. Have you ever read or heard stories from the Bible?"*

(Your turn!)

CHALLENGE 6

This week, we've learned a lot about how you can help others know Jesus. What's the *main* thing you learned this week that you don't want to forget? (Look back at the bottom lines if you need a reminder!)

_ _

_ _

We've also talked a lot about magnets. We said that just like magnets attract certain metals to themselves, we can be magnets that draw people toward Jesus.

Ready for an experiment?

Here's what you'll need:
- **Magnet**
- **Paper**
- **Pen or pencil**
- **Scissors**
- **Timer**
- **Lightweight metal object like a paperclip or small, iron nail**

Step 1
On the next page, there are two mazes, one on either side. Tear or cut out this page.

Step 2
Which maze looks harder? Maze 1 or Maze 2? _ _ _ _ _ _ _ _ _ _
Start with the maze that looks easier.

Step 3
Place the metal object at the start of the maze.

START

FINISH

Step 4
Slide the magnet under the paper, beneath the metal object.

Step 5
Now, move the metal object through the maze, using only the magnet.

Step 6
Now that you've got the hang of it, try it again. Only this time—time yourself and record your time here.

_ _ _ _ _ _ _ _

Step 7
Flip the paper to the other maze and complete the exercise again. What was your time on the second maze?

_ _ _ _ _ _ _ _

BONUS STEP
Create a maze of your own on a separate sheet of paper. See if you can make it more difficult (take longer) than the other two mazes!

Remember, **you can help others know Jesus.** You can be like a magnet that draws others to Jesus. You can do that no matter how old you are or how far along you are in your faith. You can also help others know Jesus just by being kind. And sometimes, you can help others know Jesus by telling them about Him.

There's more than one way to tell others about Jesus. Choose one to focus on the next few weeks and watch as you draw the people you care about toward the one true God!

DECODE IT!

Which country has the largest number of mazes?

WEEK 7

PAUL

SHIP-
WRECKED

ACTS 27:1-28:10

DAY 1

KNOWING JESUS CHANGES THE WAY YOU SEE YOUR PROBLEMS.

When is the last time you had a problem? Something you were worried about or bothered by? Something you had to figure out or face, but you didn't really want to? Think about it. A lost shoe. A big test. A sick family member. List a few problems, big and small, that you've faced:

1. _____

2. _____

3. _____

4. _____

5. _____

Did you know that your mind is a powerful thing? It is! In fact, your mind is more powerful than any computer known to man![1] And when your mind is faced with a problem, it works a lot like a computer . . . only better.

This week, we're going to talk about problems.

And Paul . . . Paul definitely had a problem.

Let's review what's happened with Paul so far.

- **Before Paul saw the light (literally) and became a Jesus-follower, he did not like Jesus-followers.**
- **One day, Paul was traveling to a town called Damascus and a voice spoke to him—it was Jesus. Then, Paul was blind for three days until a man named Ananias prayed for him. Paul was able to see again. And he knew without a doubt that Jesus is God's Son.**
- **Everything else about him changed. He stopped hunting down Jesus-followers and became a Jesus-follower. He traveled all over, telling as many people as possible about his faith.**

Paul has had some pretty incredible things happen to him. But what happened to Paul next is going to blow your mind.

Yes, Paul had a problem. Well, Paul had a few problems, actually. The first problem was Paul was put in jail. Why was he put in jail? The short answer is that Paul was in jail because he was a Jesus-follower. One day, while Paul was still a prisoner, it was decided that he would travel by boat across the Mediterranean Sea to stand trial.

From the beginning of the trip, Paul knew the journey wouldn't be an easy one. The wind began to blow and the waves were getting bigger and bigger and bigger. The boat struggled to stay on course. On top of *that*, the trip was taking way longer than planned and the food supply was running low. With winter and more bad weather coming, Paul was worried they'd never make it.

Paul tried to tell the ship's commander:

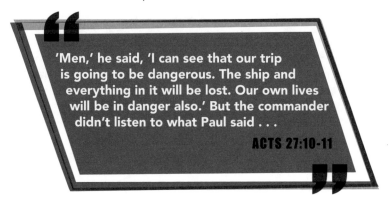

'Men,' he said, 'I can see that our trip is going to be dangerous. The ship and everything in it will be lost. Our own lives will be in danger also.' But the commander didn't listen to what Paul said . . .

ACTS 27:10-11

Paul had quite a few problems:

1. **Paul was being held as a prisoner because of his faith.**
2. **Paul was on a ship without enough food in the middle of a huge storm.**
3. **Paul knew they were in big trouble, but no one would listen.**

If you were Paul, how would you have handled all these problems? Stolen the lifeboat and paddled to safety? Hitched a ride to the nearest island on the back of a dolphin? Locked yourself under the deck and pretended you were just on a roller coaster?

-- --

-- --

-- --

Paul didn't do any of those things. Because Paul knew Jesus, it changed the way he saw his problems.

Want to know what happened? You'll have to keep reading to find out.

Spoiler alert: Paul was right!

DAY 2

WHEN YOU CHANGE YOUR FOCUS, YOUR PROBLEMS DON'T FEEL SO BIG.

Each and every day, you are faced with problems of all sizes. You can't find your bookbag, or your teacher caught you in a lie, or you forgot to tell your mom that your lunch account ran out of money. And your magnificent brain has the HUGE job of navigating through these problems.

Solving problems happens in your mind in two ways. First, you think through it—you take any old information you may have, combine it with new information, and you make a plan to solve the problem. And the second way is through your instincts—you rely on your gut feelings to help you figure it out.[2]

Take the lost bookbag for example. You could think through the problem. You think about the last place you saw the bookbag. You try and remember the places you usually leave it. And then you try and recall if you've recently seen it somewhere new. Or, you could rely on your instincts. You have a feeling you probably left it on the bus. You've almost left it there several times, and something inside you says that's where it is.

Usually, our brains combine both types of problem-solving. And most of the time, we don't even realize that it's happening!

When it came to Paul's problems—being stuck on a ship without food in the middle of a storm—his brain had already come to a solution: *stop sailing and get off the boat!* But the ship's commander wouldn't listen to him. Here's what happened next:

> Before very long, a wind blew down from the island. It had the force of a hurricane. It was called the Northeaster. The ship was caught by the storm. We could not keep it sailing into the wind. So we gave up and were driven along by the wind.
>
> **ACTS 27:14-15**

After Paul warned that the weather conditions were already dangerous, the wind and rain picked up even more. In fact, the storm had the force of a hurricane! And just like Paul said, the ship was caught in the storm. It got so bad that the crew couldn't even steer the sails. They had no choice but to let the raging waves toss and push the boat across the sea, with no direction or control.

Paul's problems got even *worse.*

DECODE IT!

Intuition, feelings, and ESP are all other ways to say which of our two problem-solving methods?

If you had been Paul, what would you have been thinking about the people in charge of the ship?
(Check all that are true for you.)

- ☐ **I told you so!**
- ☐ **I should be in charge.**
- ☐ **We're all gonna die!**
- ☐ **They should have listened to me.**
- ☐ **Things can't get any worse.**

If you checked that last response, think about it for just a minute. Is that true? Could things have been any worse for Paul?

The answer is *yes*. As big as Paul's problems were—and they were plenty big!—they could have been even bigger.

We do that in our own lives, don't we? We have a bad day, or a bad week, and we think, *This is the worst. Things couldn't get any harder.* What *is* true is that there will always be people who have problems smaller than us, and there will always be people with problems bigger than us.

One thing we can do when we're faced with a problem that feels too big is to change our focus. Instead of focusing on what's going wrong, we can choose to focus on what's going right.

Let's say you're having a bad week. A really, really bad week.

- **Your best friend embarrasses you in front of a bunch of people.**
- **You fail the vocabulary test you studied so hard for.**
- **Your parents get into a huge fight and scream at each other.**

Don't get me wrong—all of these are real problems. They hurt. And when you combine all of them into one week, it can definitely feel like things can't get any worse. But what if you changed your focus?

You remind yourself that:

- **Your best friend didn't embarrass you on purpose.**
- **You did well on all the other vocabulary tests, so your overall average isn't bad.**
- **You know your parents love you no matter what.**

Our problems are only as big as we allow them to be.

Look back at Day 1. You listed 5 problems you were recently faced with. Rewrite those problems below with a different focus.

1. _____

2. _____

3. _____

4. _____

5. _____

Your problems are real. They hurt and they matter. But no matter how bad your problems seem, when you change your focus, your problems don't feel quite as big.

DAY 3

WE CAN HAVE FAITH IN THE MIDDLE OF OUR PROBLEMS.

When our brain senses that we are facing a big problem, it goes into superhero mode. It sends messages to different parts of our bodies that help us handle whatever we're facing. One of those signals tells our bodies to produce a chemical called cortisol. Now, cortisol is some pretty amazing stuff. It helps the brain slow down so it can think clearly. It also sends energy to important muscles and increases your heart rate and breathing.[3] All of this happens without you even realizing it so that you have the best chance of conquering any problem that comes your way.

But there's something else you can depend on—*Someone* else. And it's even more powerful and more dependable than cortisol. And it was all Paul had when his problems got even bigger!

Remember, Paul was held prisoner on a ship that was being torn apart by a terrible storm. The commander of the ship wouldn't listen to Paul's warnings, and then the weather got worse. The crew lost control and the ship was tossed around in the sea like it was a bath toy.

Here's what happened next:

> . . . We almost lost the lifeboat that was tied to the side of the ship. So the men lifted the lifeboat on board. Then they tied ropes under the ship itself to hold it together. They were afraid it would get stuck on the sandbars of Syrtis. So they lowered the sea anchor and let the ship be driven along. We took a very bad beating from the storm. The next day the crew began to throw the ship's contents overboard. On the third day, they even threw the ship's tools and supplies overboard with their own hands. The sun and stars didn't appear for many days. The storm was terrible. So we gave up all hope of being saved.
>
> **ACTS 27:16-20**

Things weren't looking good for Paul and his shipmates. They were so worried about sinking that they threw all their supplies and tools overboard . . . everything they needed to survive. They hadn't eaten for many days and the skies stayed black and dark. Everyone lost hope of being saved.

But Paul hadn't lost hope because Paul still had his faith.

> 'Now I beg you to be brave. Not one of you will die. Only the ship will be destroyed. I belong to God and serve him. Last night his angel stood beside me. The angel said, "Do not be afraid, Paul. You must go on trial in front of Caesar. God has shown his grace by sparing the lives of all those sailing with you." Men, continue to be brave. I have faith in God. It will happen just as he told me.'
>
> **ACTS 27:22-25**

Paul had a message for the hopeless people on his ship: God promised it would be okay. God keeps His promises. So we will be okay.

Paul had his faith. He knew that God was with him and that no matter how bad things looked, God always keeps His promises.

DECODE IT!

The body produces what chemical when it senses danger?

The same is true for you. You can look at any problem in your life—no matter how big or how small—and you can know that God is with you. You can have faith that even when things look bad—really, really bad—God always keeps His promises.

If there's a problem you're facing right now, spend a few minutes talking to God about it. Tell Him how you're feeling. Then tell Him you want to have faith like Paul—that you want to believe His promises are true, even when your problems feel really big.

DAY 4

WHEN WE HAVE FAITH, IT HELPS OTHERS FACE THEIR PROBLEMS.

Have you ever had someone try to copy you? Had someone start dressing like you, talking like you, and liking the things that you like? Maybe a friend at school got his hair cut just like yours, or your little sister started to love professional soccer after she heard you talking about it.

Did you know that you can actually become like the people you spend the most time with? It's true. Your brain rewires itself to think like those people, talk like those people, and act like those people. This actually has a name. It's called the "social proximity effect".[4]

Basically, the social proximity effect says that you will become a lot like the people you spend the most time with. We will pick up on their habits, words, preferences, and sometimes, we will pick up on their faith.

Listen to what happened to Paul and the other men on his boat after they'd been lost at sea for two weeks . . .

> Just before dawn Paul tried to get them all to eat. 'For the last 14 days,' he said, 'you have wondered what would happen. You have gone without food. You haven't eaten anything. Now I am asking you to eat some food. You need it to live. Not one of you will lose a single hair from your head.' After Paul said this, he took some bread and gave thanks to God. He did this where they all could see him. Then he broke it and began to eat. All of them were filled with hope.
>
> **Acts 27:33-36**

The soldiers on the ship were faced with problems that seemed too big to overcome. They had no supplies, no tools, and were on board a damaged ship with no rescue in sight. They hadn't eaten in 14 days, and I'm sure they were all extremely afraid. But most of all, they were hopeless.

But Paul continued to have faith. For two longs weeks, he continued to believe that God was with him and that God keeps His promises. He encouraged the men, telling them that since God had promised they'd be okay, not a single hair on anyone's head would be harmed. Paul prayed and thanked God right there in front of them, for all to see.

And do you know what happened? Social proximity effect happened. Soon, the men started to believe Paul. They started to believe like Paul and eventually they were filled with hope.

And eventually, that hope turned into gratitude, because they were all saved. They all made it to an island and were greeted by its kind inhabitants who treated them well and nursed them back to health.

Not one person lost their life. God kept His promise.

Did you know that when you have faith during your hard times, it can help others have faith during their hard times? You can be a positive influence in someone's life, just by believing that God keeps His promises.

Here are three things Paul did during his hard time to help others during their hard time:

1. **You can tell others that God keeps His promises.**
   It can be hard to know what to say to someone who is hurting, especially if you're hurting, too. But you can always remind them that God is a good, loving God, and that He is always with us, even when it feels like He's not.

2. **You can have hope.**
   You can be positive when everything feels negative. Saying things like, "God's got this," and "I'm here for you," seems small, but it can go a long way to change someone's attitude when they're down.

3. **You can pray.**
   Paul prayed out loud where everyone could hear him. You don't have to pray out loud if that makes you nervous or uncomfortable, but you can tell someone that you're praying for them . . . but then don't forget to actually do it!

From the list of those three things, which will be the easiest thing for you to do to help a friend when you're both faced with a problem?

- -

- -

- -

Which will be the most challenging?

- -

- -

- -

Spend a couple of minutes talking to God. Ask Him to help you have faith during your hard times. Remember, when you're going through a hard time, your faith could be the very thing that helps someone get through their own hard time.

CHALLENGE 7

This week, we've learned a lot about how your faith changes the way you see your problems. What's the *main* thing you learned this week that you don't want to forget? (Look back at the bottom lines if you need a reminder!)

_____

_____

Today's experiment is all about your brain encountering different problems. These problems are riddles. See how many you can answer without using your decoder.

Here's what you'll need:

- **Pen or pencil**
- **Focus Decoder**

RIDDLE #1

How far can a fox run into the woods?

RIDDLE #2

Which word
is spelled wrong
in every dictionary?

RIDDLE #3

I am an odd number.
Take away a letter
and I become even.
What am I?

RIDDLE #4

How many months
have 28 days
in them?

RIDDLE #5

What gets bigger and bigger the more you take away from it?

RIDDLE #6

Forward I am heavy, but backward I am not. What am I?

RIDDLE #7

What has 88 keys, but can't open a single door?

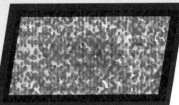

RIDDLE #8

If you took two apples from three apples, how many would you have?

How did your brain do handling all those problems? Did having the Focus Decoder make you feel more confident, knowing you'd have the answer if you couldn't figure it out on your own?

Our bottom line this week is **knowing Jesus changes the way you see your problems.** Did you know that you actually have a Focus Decoder in life? It's the Bible. It has all God's words in it—things He wants you to know and believe and do. The next time you feel stuck, try reading some of it. You can open it randomly, but it might be helpful to look back at some of the verses we've talked about over the last few weeks.

WEEK 4

HEAVEN

ALL THINGS

NEW

DAY 1

FOLLOWING JESUS WILL TURN OUT GREATER THAN YOU CAN IMAGINE.

Are you one of those people who loves storms? Maybe you're fascinated by thunder and lightning, and your dad has to tell you to stop staring out the windows when the weather is particularly bad?

Or do you hate storms? Maybe the sound of thunder makes your armpits sweat and the sight of lightning makes your stomach do cartwheels?

How do you feel about storms?

- -

- -

At Saturn's north pole, there's a storm that's always raging. And it's not a small storm, either. Saturn's weather system is double the size of Earth! In other words, the size of the *storm* is twice as big as the planet Earth! And it remains one of the biggest mysteries ever. Why? Because the storm is shaped like a perfect hexagon.[1]

If you're not sure what that shape looks like, you're about to draw one on the next page. Connect the dots with straight lines!

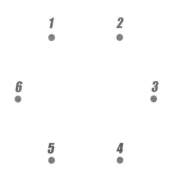

Maybe you've never paid that much attention to the weather on the news or checked out storms on The Weather Channel App, but storms are never, not ever, under any circumstances, in the shape of a hexagon. On top of that, hexagons only occur in nature in crystal form. Scientists have no idea how or why Saturn's massive storm came to be shaped this way. To make matters even *more* confusing, the storm appears to have changed colors from turquoise to yellow. [2]

Pretty weird, right?

This is just one example of something scientists know *a lot* about, but not *everything* about . . . not yet, anyway. There are still plenty of researchers working daily to figure it out.

Scientists know a lot about . . . well, a lot. But they don't know everything. There are many mysteries that occur in nature that we'll never have the answers to. The same is true for what happens when our life on Earth is finished.

Yikes—that's not a super fun topic, is it? But maybe that's because we don't have all the answers about what happens next.

But the Bible does tell us *some* things. Some important things. And one of those things is that everyone in God's family is promised life in heaven.

The book we're reading from this week is called Revelation which was written by John, a Jesus-follower. Any guesses as to what the word Relevation means?

- -

Revelation basically means *made known*. And in the book of Revelation, many truths about the mysteries of heaven are made known. Like this:

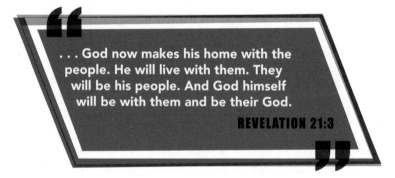

> . . . God now makes his home with the people. He will live with them. They will be his people. And God himself will be with them and be their God.
>
> **REVELATION 21:3**

We're going to talk a lot about heaven during this last week together. But first, think about this . . .

If you could ask one question about heaven, what would it be?

- -

- -

Life with God and the rest of His family sounds incredible. It sounds too good to be true! But it is true. So, what does it take to get to heaven?

Kindness?
Goodness?
Forgiveness?

Actually, no. As difficult as getting into heaven may sound, it's actually very simple. What do you think it takes to get into heaven?

- -

- -

Ready for another big reveal?

All you need to do to to get into heaven is to *follow Jesus*. That doesn't mean you have to be perfect—no one is perfect. All you need is a relationship with God's Son. **Following Jesus will turn out greater than you can imagine** because it's our faith that gives us the hope of heaven.

Want to uncover more truths about the mystery of heaven? Meet me back here tomorrow!

Which planet has the "The Great Red Spot"— the biggest storm in our solar system?

DAY 2

IN HEAVEN, THERE IS NO MORE SADNESS.

Let's talk about treasure. Buried treasure, to be exact. If you had to bury a treasure somewhere, where would you bury it and why?

- -

- -

Okay, most of us don't have any actual *treasure*. But we do have things we value. Take your tablet, for example. Or your favorite book. Or the basketball jersey you got for Christmas last year. We all have things that are meaningful to us, even if they aren't considered "treasures."

In 1952, a scroll was found by archaeologists in a cave.[3] There are a few reasons this scroll was mysterious. One, while most scrolls are made of parchment paper, this one was made of metal—mostly copper. Two, the scroll was about 2,000 years old. And three (I saved the best for last), the scroll records a HUGE, MEGA, MAJOR amount of hidden silver and gold.

Scientists *still* don't know if the treasure is real. And, if it is real, no one knows where it could be found.[4]

There's a good chance we'll never know the answer to either of those questions, but it's pretty cool to imagine being the person who strikes it rich by discovering all that silver and gold.

In our first session, we talked a little about heaven. We said that there is a lot about heaven that remains a mystery to us. But there are some things we do know:

1. **Following Jesus gives us the hope of heaven.**
2. **God will be with us, living with us in heaven.**

Let's see what else we can uncover:

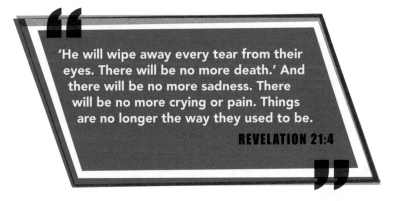

'He will wipe away every tear from their eyes. There will be no more death.' And there will be no more sadness. There will be no more crying or pain. Things are no longer the way they used to be.

REVELATION 21:4

We just learned something extremely cool about heaven. There won't be any more death, sadness, crying, or pain!

Wow. Just, wow.

Let's continue.

In the book of Revelation, John says, "Things are no longer the way they used to be." In other words, all the things that make you sad, that hurt you . . . they won't exist in heaven. Heaven will be a place of joy, a place of peace, and a place of *good*.

That sounds pretty awesome. Way more awesome than a buried treasure!

The next time something happens and you think, "If God loves us, why did this happen?" remember this—God is a good God. And once we're with Him in heaven, we won't have to hurt or see the people we care about hurt ever again.

Spend a few minutes talking to God. Tell Him your thoughts on heaven. You can also ask Him questions you may have about heaven—or anything, really. God wants us to tell Him what we're thinking, even if that means admitting we're not sure what we think or believe.

DECODE IT!

In 1992, British farmer Peter Whatling lost his hammer in a field. Instead of finding it, he found actual buried treasure! Any guesses how much it was worth?

DAY 3

JESUS MAKES ALL THINGS NEW.

When is the last time you got something new? Maybe it was a backpack for school, or a keychain for your birthday, or even a bike last Christmas. Think, and then draw a picture of it below.

What kind of words do we use to describe something new?

- **Shiny**
- **Clean**
- **Fresh**
- **Perfect**

Now, think of a few words on your own. What words would you use to describe the "new" thing you drew?

-

-

-

Check this out—in 2015, people in Canada noticed strange lights in the sky that had never been reported before.[5] As it turns out, these lights were actually a new aurora. An aurora is a natural light display that shimmers in the sky. They are only visible at night, and usually only appear in places closer to the North or South Poles.[6] These people got excited—which got other people excited, too. Eventually, NASA got involved and the new, shimmery light display was named STEVE—Strong Thermal Emission Velocity. (I prefer Steve.)

New stuff is cool, right? It's fun! It's thrilling!

And in heaven, everything will be new—even us. Listen to this:

He who was sitting on the throne said, 'I am making everything new!'

REVELATION 21:5a

In the book of Revelation, John tells us in the end, all things will be made new. What things? *Everything.* Let's add that to the list of things we know about heaven:

1. **Following Jesus gives us the hope of heaven.**
2. **God will be living with us in heaven.**
3. **Everything will be made new.**

Look back at the words we use to describe new things.

- **Shiny**
- **Clean**
- **Fresh**
- **Perfect**

In heaven, everything will be all those things—everything will be made new. How amazing is that?

DAY 4

YOU CAN TRUST WHAT GOD SAYS.

Do you like mysteries? What's your favorite mystery book, movie, or show?

- -

- -

Have you ever encountered a mystery of your own? Like, where *do* all the matches to our socks go? The thing about mysteries is that we can have a feeling we know the truth, but unless there's a big reveal at the end, we don't really know for sure.

You might be wondering why we're talking about this now, after we've spent this whole week uncovering the mysteries of heaven. But here's the thing about faith . . . part of having faith means that we are okay not knowing *everything*. We are okay having a few questions unanswered until the big reveal at the end—heaven.

Here's another mystery for you.

In the 1930's, Amelia Earhart was quickly becoming one of the world's most famous pilots. In 1935, she became the first person to fly from Hawaii to California. Along with this great accomplishment, Amelia also became the first person to fly alone over the Atlantic *and* Pacific Oceans. It was no wonder then, that in June of 1937, Amelia set out to become the first female to fly around the world.[7]

Everything seemed to be going well for the pilot until July 2. She was over half-way done with her flight when suddenly . . . she vanished. Gone. Immediately, people started looking for Amelia and her plane. But searches on land, air, and sea turned up with *nothing*.[8]

Some people think Amelia had an emergency landing and became a castaway on an island. Others think she was captured by Japanese spies. Some think she wanted to become super-duper famous, so she disappeared on purpose, for attention.

What happened to Amelia Earhart is one of the biggest mysteries of the last 100 years.

Mysteries are fascinating to us. But they also make us long to know the truth.

Speaking of truth, let's uncover one last mystery of heaven together.

In John's vision, the One sitting on the throne said this:

'Write this down. You can trust these words. They are true.'

REVELATION 21:5b

In that verse, we uncover the most important part of the mystery of heaven: *you can trust these words.*

You can trust what God says. You can trust that Jesus is His one and only Son, sent to Earth so that we could be in God's family forever. When we encounter a mystery—whether it be a mystery of heaven or a mystery in our lives right now—we can trust in God. We can follow Jesus. We can know that no matter what, God loves us and Jesus wants to be our friend forever. We can have faith.

And based on the little we've learned about heaven so far, it sounds like following Jesus will turn out greater than you ever imagined.

DECODE IT!

Amelia Earhart's nickname was...?

CHALLENGE 8

This week, we've learned a lot about how following Jesus will turn out greater than we can imagine. What's the *main* thing you learned this week that you don't want to forget? (Look back at the bottom lines if you need a refresher!)

- -

- -

Here's what you need:

- **Sheet of paper**
- **Markers, pencil, or colored pencils**

In the space provided, draw a picture of what you think heaven will look like. Make sure to include:

- **Where you'll live**
- **Who will be there**
- **What you'll do**
- **How you'll feel**

(Since no one really knows *for sure*, there is no right or wrong response.)

Now, take your sheet of paper and ask someone else to draw what they think heaven will be like. Don't show them your drawing, but tell them to include the same things you did.

When they're done, compare your drawings.

How are they the same?

How are they different?

Whether you drew flying cars, unmeltable ice cream, or beds made of cotton candy, here's the coolest thing about heaven: It's going to be even better than your wildest dreams. You can imagine some pretty great stuff, but **following Jesus will turn out greater than you can imagine.** That's true in your life now, and in your life in heaven.

I HAVE QUESTIONS

If you're reading this, it probably means that you have some questions about faith.

First of all, go ahead and pat yourself on the back. Give yourself a high-five and a fist-bump. You're taking a huge step toward Jesus by reading this book—and especially by reading these pages.

Having a relationship with Jesus may sound strange to you. Or confusing. Or impossible, even. That's okay. It's really very simple.

But there are a few things you should know.

When God created the world and everything in it, God saw that it was good. Like, 100 percent-all-the-way-perfectly-good. But then something happened. The first humans God created—Adam and Eve—they sinned. They broke the one rule that God had given them. And when they broke that rule, things weren't 100 percent-all-the-way-perfectly-good anymore.

Sin is the stuff we do that's wrong. We all sin. You sin. I sin. Even parents, teachers, and pastors sin!

One big problem with sin is that it separates us from God.

Have you ever been in the complete dark before? If you can, find a room without windows in your house right now. Maybe a bathroom or a closet. Before you turn off the light and shut the door, read these questions to think about:

1. What's it feel like to be in the dark for a long time?

2. How do you know where to go when you're in the dark?

3. What's the one thing you wish you had when you're in the dark (besides a snack!)

Okay—now you're ready! Go into a dark place and think about that for a few minutes. If you want, you can come out and check the questions to make sure you've covered them all. When you're finished, come back to this page.

Being surrounded by complete darkness all the time would be miserable, right? You don't know which way to go—you may even be afraid to move one inch!

When we're separated from God by our sin, it's like being in the dark. But when we're in God's family, we have access to the brightest light ever —Jesus! When we walk with God to grow our faith in His Son, we can face our problems and fears with confidence and focus.

So, how do we do that? How do we move from being in the darkness of sin into the light of God? Well, we can't do anything about our sin, because we're humans. But God loves us so much that He designed the perfect plan.

God gave us the most valuable, precious, and perfect thing He could—He sent His son Jesus to live on Earth. Jesus lived a perfect life—He never sinned. Then, He gave up his life when he died on the cross.

Three days later, Jesus rose from the dead, proving He is God's Son! Then, He went back to heaven to live with God forever.

When we tell God that we believe Jesus is His Son and ask forgiveness for our sins, we receive an amazing gift. We get to have a relationship with God that will last forever. We move from living in darkness to living in the light!

Have you ever made the decision to believe in Jesus and all He did for you? If not, talk to someone you trust (maybe the person who gave you this book). Ask that what it means to have a relationship with Jesus. Then, tell them you're ready to have a faith of your own.

ENDNOTES

Week One

1. allabouteyes.com/best-eyes-animal-kingdom

2. space.com/dwarf-planet-haumea-ring-shape.html

3. space.com/23091-haumea.html

4. space.com/19103-milky-way-100-billion-planets.html

5. healthline.com/health/how-to-check-heart-rate

6. healthline.com/health/fun-facts-about-the-heart

7. masterclass.com/articles/music-101-what-are-musical-notes-learn-more-about-how-to-read-music

8. sciencekidsathome.com/science_topics/what_is_sound.html

9. livescience.com/14395-science-music-ria.html

10. Aristophanes, *The Clouds*, 765-70.

Week Two

1. sweye.com/blog/optical-care/interesting-facts-about-eyes/

2. natgeokids.com/nz/discover/science/general-science/human-eye

3. allaboutvision.com/conditions/dilated-pupils.htm

4. nei.nih.gov/learn-about-eye-health/nei-for-kids/cool-eye-tricks

Week Three

1. kidshealth.org/en/kids/afraid.html

2. kidshealth.org/en/kids/afraid.html

3. kidshealth.org/en/teens/phobias.html

4. mentalfloss.com/article/25525/quick-10-10-people-photographic-memories

5. guinnessworldrecords.com/world-records/67743-fastest-time-to-memorize-and-recall-a-deck-of-playing-cards

6. bestlifeonline.com/facts-about-memory

7. pi-world-ranking-list.com/index.php?page=lists&category=pi

Week Four

1. kids.frontiersin.org/article/10.3389/frym.2013.00005

2. sciencedaily.com/releases/2017/06/170606090936.htm

3. brainfacts.org/thinking-sensing-and-behaving/emotions-stress-and-anxiety/2018/do-hurt-feelings-actually-hurt-010518

Week Five

1. indiatimes.com/technology/science-and-future/13-incredible-inventions-that-will-power-the-future-and-change-our-tomorrow-for-the-best-275894.html

2. glasseshistory.com

3. cnbc.com/2017/09/20/these-amazing-electronic-glasses-help-the-legally-blind-see.html

Week Six

1. magnet-shop.com/magnets-throughout-the-history

2. nationalgeographic.org/encyclopedia/magnetism

3. scienceforkidsclub.com/earths-magnetism.html

4. scienceforkidsclub.com/earths-magnetism.html

5. dkfindout.com/us/science/magnets/poles-magnet

6. medium.com/the-space-perspective/the-most-powerful-magnets-in-the-universe-magnetars-4ae54162d723

7. solomon.as.utexas.edu/magnetar.html

Week Seven

1. newscientist.com/article/dn9970-faq-the-human-brain

2. newscientist.com/article/dn9970-faq-the-human-brain/#ixzz650K7tj6F

3. kids.frontiersin.org/article/10.3389/frym.2017.00071

4. riskology.co/proximity-effect

Week Eight

1. solarsystem.nasa.gov/missions/cassini/science/saturn/hexagon-in-motion

2. businessinsider.com/phenomena-science-cant-explain-2019-1#no-one-knows-why-saturns-north-pole-has-a-swirling-hexagon-shaped-storm-3

3. livescience.com/11361-history-overlooked-mysteries.html

4. ancient-origins.net/news/lost-treasure-dead-sea-copper-scroll-001457

5. businessinsider.com/biggest-scientific-discoveries-of-2018-2018-12#star-gazers-spotted-a-new-kind-of-aurora-that-travels-farther-south-than-most-its-name-is-steve-4

6. nationalgeographic.org/encyclopedia/aurora

7. ameliaearhartmuseum.org/AmeliaEarhart/AEBiography.htm

8. biography.com/explorer/amelia-earhart